Diagnosing Dyslexia

guide to the assessment

Cynthia Klein

The
Basic Skills
Agency

Acknowledgements

I would like to thank the following:

Alexandra Davies for reading everything so carefully and giving always useful advice

Helen Sunderland for her encouragement and helpful notes on miscue analysis

Alison Swabey for her Irregular Word List and for her ever thoughtful and excellent suggestions for clarifying potential misunderstandings

Christina Hansford for letting me use her diagnostic report and take some liberties with it

Steve McSweeney for helping to update me on special examination provision

All the students I have worked with and tutors I have taught who have helped me to think about dyslexia and how best to understand and diagnose it

The Basic Skills Agency for giving me the opportunity to improve this book.

© The Basic Skills Agency, Commonwealth House, 1–19 New Oxford Street, London, WC1A 1NU. Tel: 020 7405 4017 Fax: 020 7440 6626
e-mail: enquiries@basic-skills.co.uk www.basic-skills.co.uk

ISBN 1 85990 264 2

Design: Studio 21

First edition published March 1993

Second edition printed September 2003

Contents

Introduction
to Second Edition

Since the writing of the first edition, there have been many changes in the world of dyslexia. When I first wrote this book, there was little research or literature on adults. Since then, demand to know more about dyslexia in adults has grown enormously and there are now many books on the subject. Research in dyslexia has given us many more insights into the difficulties from a neurological and cognitive perspective.   ·

However, the greatest change lies in the growing awareness of the numbers and needs of dyslexic adults reflected in policy and legislation. Dyslexic adults in education are now included in legislation for learners with disabilities.

The Further and Higher Education Act of 1992, for the first time, put into legislation further education colleges' responsibility to have regard to students with learning difficulties and disabilities; this was backed up by specific funding for additional learning support and by the influential Tomlinson committee's report, *Inclusive Learning*, in 1996.

The Learning and Skills Act 2000 gives the Learning and Skills Council a duty 'to have due regard to promote equality of opportunity between disabled and non-disabled learners'. The SEN (Special Educational Needs) and Disability Act 2001 has brought education under the Disability Discrimination Act; for the first time, learners with disabilities have legal rights in terms of their access to post-school education. This means post-16 education providers have a duty not to treat disabled people less favourably than others and to make reasonable adjustments when they are put at a substantial disadvantage. It requires providers to be anticipatory and proactive in encouraging people to disclose their disability.

Some disabilities are visible; dyslexia is not. If a learner has not disclosed a disability she might not be able to prove she has been discriminated against.

However, the organisation does have to take 'reasonable steps' to encourage disclosure.

Many dyslexic adults will not have had their difficulties previously identified and therefore not realise they have a disability to disclose. Consequently, it is important that staff in the institution are able to recognise such difficulties and that these learners are offered opportunities for a specialist diagnostic assessment.

The first edition of this book came out of a national project for basic skills tutors. At the time we started the project in 1990, the existence of 'dyslexia' was still questioned by some, as was the existence of significant numbers dyslexic adults in basic skills classes. Now, the Government's *Skills for Life* national strategy for improving adult literacy and numeracy, recognises dyslexia as a significant factor for some adults in their difficulty acquiring literacy and numeracy skills, and addresses this. A dyslexia literacy module that may be used as a screening tool is included in the *Skills for Life* diagnostic assessment materials, and guidance for supporting dyslexic learners is included in the learning materials and in *Access for All* (see Resources).

Current research

Essentially, the indicators of dyslexia and profiles of dyslexic learners have not changed since the first edition; what has changed is that research into brain organisation and functioning has given us a greater understanding of the underlying factors and has helped us build better models of it. We know that dyslexia has a hereditary component and that it has a basis in the brain (Frith, 1999; Galaburda, 1999). Some research suggests that dyslexic individuals are slower in perceptual processing; they have problems processing rapid changes in auditory or visual stimuli so they cannot discriminate rapidly changing sounds (Tallal et al, 1997) or easily process visual sequences of letters (Stein, 2001). Other research points to the role of the cerebellum and underlying faulty automatisation of skills; this puts more emphasis on the role of motor integration in dyslexia (Nicolson and Fawcett, 1999). There also continues to be increasing evidence that phonological processing difficulties, i.e. problems processing speech sounds, are a major underlying factor in dyslexia (Frith, 1999; Snowling, 2001).

More research into dyslexic adults, although still fairly sparse, has led to a greater acknowledgement of different patterns of difficulties among adults. For instance, studies have confirmed that while some dyslexic adults have the phonological processing difficulties which commonly characterise dyslexia, others have difficulties processing visual sequences (Boden and Brodeur, 1999) and/or suffer from visual stress (Wilkins, 1995) or their primary difficulty appears to be visual-motor coordination (Rack, 1997).

Diagnosis of adults

Also, since the first edition, much greater numbers of dyslexic adults are being diagnosed and the principle of diagnosis by specialist teachers has been accepted within education and by examination boards. Consequently, there has been a more explicit debate on the methodology suitable for diagnosing adults and requirements for those eligible to write reports for special examination provision.

In order to write a diagnostic report for the purposes of examination provision, teachers need to have a qualification recognised by the Joint Council for General Qualifications. At the time of writing, there is no clear guidance on reports for applications for the Disabled Student Allowance for higher education.

However, with all these developments, the original aims of diagnosis for teachers and learners (from the first edition) remain:

- **An educational diagnosis is an integral part of determining a learner's educational needs. Many adults and young people in further and adult education have never had their specific difficulties diagnosed at school and have, therefore, absorbed confused and confusing messages about their ability to learn. To become successful learners they need to understand their difficulties and the implication of these for learning.**

- **Tutors and lecturers also may be confused by the dyslexic learner whose consistent underachievement seems due to what may look like laziness, carelessness or inability to handle course content. Understanding a learner's specific difficulties and how these may affect the learner's classroom performance can enable the tutor or lecturer to adopt teaching methods and strategies that help the dyslexic learner to succeed.**

It is worth reiterating that the diagnosis is essentially for the dyslexic adults themselves, to help them make sense of their past and to be a light to a brighter future.

Methodology

The diagnostic methodology is based on what I believe is the best practice for teachers offered by current thinking and knowledge on diagnosing adults. Standardised tests are not used here as they are rarely standardised beyond the age of 17 or 18, so are not reliable for adults, and are rarely standardised on a multicultural sample. There are some more recent standardised tests which may be helpful for tutors and may be needed for examination purposes (see Turner, 1997) but there is not full agreement among experts on the use of standardised tests with adults. As well as being unreliable because of adults' compensatory strategies, they also do not identify some of the most persistent and problematic areas for adults, such as organisational and handwriting difficulties. Nor are reading and spelling ages used here as they are demeaning and humiliating to adult learners and give little meaningful information or indication as to the kind of difficulty and its *effects* on the learner's reading, writing and spelling at the relevant level.

The methodology aims for a *qualitative* analysis of difficulties, rather than a quantitative one. Not only does this give more information about the learner's difficulties, but it is more appropriate to the nature of dyslexia, which is both individual and persistent at all levels of literacy. Thus, students in higher education may continue to reveal such difficulties although they can cope with advanced reading and writing demands when given ample time and helped to develop appropriate strategies for study.

The methodology includes:

- **an in-depth interview including a learning history and profile of areas of difficulty and strength**

- **a miscue analysis of reading, including reading style and comprehension, reinforced by single word and non-word reading**

- a spelling error analysis from a diagnostic dictation
- an analysis of one or more pieces of free writing
- additional tasks, including a 'spoonerism' (phonological segmentation) task.

Other tasks not included but which are easily available, such as a digit span task (see Resources), are useful additions.

A period of appropriate tuition before a full diagnostic assessment is helpful in giving the tutor a sense of the learner's difficulties and learning style; and if necessary, a period of time working with the learner after the diagnosis may clarify or confirm the nature of the difficulties.

Although guidelines are given for using materials in this book, a specialist training course in teaching and diagnosing dyslexic adults is recommended for making full and accurate use of these materials.

For a more extended discussion on the issues in diagnosing dyslexic adults and a model of diagnosis for adults, see Chapter 2 in Morgan and Klein, 2000.

Notes on the changes to the first edition

I have tried to keep the feel of the original while bringing it up-to-date. I have made some modifications to the methodology and small changes in emphasis on the basis of my own and my colleagues' experience in diagnosing dyslexic adults, in order to clarify points and make it more useful. I have also made some corrections in the coding of the Miscue Analysis illustration and tried to give better examples or explanations throughout where the originals were misleading or weak. I have made some modifications to Chapter 9 to take more account of current thinking. I have kept the original illustrations except for the report which is more recent and uses more additional tasks. I have also added a simpler irregular word list and a 'spoonerism' task, along with additional questions or suggestions to reflect new knowledge about dyslexia and to fill gaps which have become apparent.

I have not rewritten Appendix 1 on the reading process (though I have made some small amendments) because I believe the dual-route, cascaded model of reading (see Jackson and Coltheart, 2001 for an up-to-date version) is still the best for helping to make sense of the different problems that dyslexic readers may experience and how they may compensate for these. Current models may be somewhat more sophisticated, but are not essentially different.

I have made some changes in terminology. 'Dyslexia' is used in preference to 'specific learning difficulties' as 'dyslexia' is used in disability legislation and policy documents which concern adults. Dyslexic adults also prefer the name and, as with other disability groups, should have a say in what they are called.

I have replaced 'student' with 'learner' to reflect the broad base of contexts, including work-based learning, where this book may be used.

As in the original, I have used 'her' as a general pronoun when referring to the learner. This is a convention only, to make the text less awkward.

I hope this new edition will continue to support tutors in carrying out a diagnostic assessment which is a rewarding experience for both them and their dyslexic adult learners.

References

Boden, C. and Brodeur, D., 'Visual processing of verbal and non-visual stimuli in adolescents with reading disabilities', *Journal of Learning Disabilities* 32 (1), 1999.

Frith, U., 'Paradoxes in the definition of dyslexia', *Dyslexia*, Vol. 5, No. 4, 1999.

Galaburda, A., 'Developmental dyslexia: a multilevel syndrome', *Dyslexia*, Vol. 5, No. 4, 1999.

Jackson, N.E. and Coltheart, M., *Routes to Reading Success and Failure*, USA: Psychology Press, 2001.

Morgan, E. and Klein, C., *The Dyslexic Adult in a Non-dyslexic World*, Whurr, 2000.

Nicolson, R. and Fawcett, A., 'Developmental dyslexia: the role of the cerebellum', *Dyslexia*, Vol. 5, No. 3, 1999.

Rack, J., 'Issues in the assessment of developmental dyslexia in adults', *Journal of Research in Reading* 20 (1), 1997.

Shaywitz, S., 'Dyslexia', *Scientific American*, November 1996.

Snowling, M., Nation, K., Moxham, P., Gallagher, A. and Frith, U., 'Phonological processing skills of dyslexic students in higher education: a preliminary report', *Journal of Research in Reading, Special Issue: Dyslexia in Literate Adults*, Vol. 20, No. 1, 1997.

Snowling, M., 'From language to reading and dyslexia', *Dyslexia*, Vol. 7, No. 1, January–March, 2001.

Stein, J., 'The magnocellular theory of developmental dyslexia', *Dyslexia*, Vol. 7, No. 1, January–March, 2001.

Tallal, P., Miller, S.L., Jenkins, W.M. and Merzenich, M.M., 'The role of temporal processing in developmental language-based learning disorders: research and clinical implications', in B.A. Blachman (ed.) *Foundations of Reading Acquisition and Dyslexia*, Lawrence Erlbaum Assoc., 1997.

Turner, M., *Psychological Assessment of Dyslexia*, London: Whurr, 1997.

Wilkins, A., *Visual Stress*, Oxford University Press, 1995.

1 | Guide to Diagnostic Assessment

The aims of the diagnostic assessment are to determine:

- **the nature of the learner's difficulties and whether these indicate dyslexia**

- **the learner's processing (auditory, visual, motor) and cognitive strengths and weaknesses**

- **how these are manifested in reading, writing, spelling and attendant problems**

- **recommendations for helping the learner.**

For dyslexic adults, the diagnosis is an important starting point. It enables them to slough off old, internalised labels of 'stupid', 'lazy', 'thick', and to unpack their difficulties and appreciate their strengths.

The procedure involves an in-depth interview along with additional tasks, a miscue analysis of reading, including reading style and comprehension, single word and non-word reading, an analysis of a piece of free writing and an error analysis on a spelling dictation.

Preparation for the assessment includes establishing reasons for the referral and preparing the learner for the diagnosis.

Reasons for the referral should be explored with the referring tutor or other referring person to determine the appropriateness of the referral. Observations by experienced teachers can be very instructive, and can be useful later if they are involved in subsequent teaching. Indicators of the likelihood of dyslexia or related difficulty include a discrepancy between learners' evident understanding or oral abilities and their written language performance, the persistence of difficulties in acquiring the skills of reading, writing and/or spelling and other patterns of difficulty in learning which might suggest language processing problems.

The learner should be well prepared for the diagnosis so it is important that the person referring explains the purpose of the diagnosis and the reasons for it. It can be distressing if the learner is not clear about the purpose and reasons for the diagnosis or feels it is something being done *to* her rather than *with* her. The learner should be a *full participant* in the entire process.

The tutor doing the diagnosis should explain to the learner exactly what the procedure consists of and talk through any anxieties or uncertainties the learner may have; for example, about reading aloud. The tutor should also explain what will happen after the diagnostic session stress the confidential nature of the assessment, and be clear that the learner consents to it.

It is useful if the learner is asked to bring with them a piece of writing done without the use of a dictionary or help with the spelling. If appropriate, this should be a first draft of a piece of writing done as a course assignment or something written for work; a final draft of the writing is helpful for comparisons. If the learner will be taking written exams, a piece of writing under timed conditions will also be useful for comparisons.

The role of feedback is crucial to the diagnosis being a constructive experience for the learner. A feedback session should be arranged with the individual, preferably the following week, after the tutor has had time to analyse the results and draft a report. Dyslexic adults need an opportunity to have the results explained, to ask questions and to deal with the emotional impact of the diagnosis. They also need to understand the report and agree to it so they can 'own' it. They may need additional time to digest the contents of the report and the feedback, so another session may be needed to allow for this.

It is important to remember the following when carrying out a diagnostic assessment:

- *Listen* to the person you are assessing – both what they say and how they say it, and what is 'behind' the words.

- *Observe* their learning style – difficulties and strengths.

- Do not make *assumptions* about the reasons for learning failure.

2 | The Diagnostic Interview

An in-depth interview forms the basis of the diagnosis. Adults can often give a detailed history and description of their difficulties, such as memorising, sequencing and fine motor coordination. This makes it unnecessary to give batteries of tests. It also enables the individual being diagnosed to be a full partner in the diagnostic process and to begin to uncover their strengths as well as their weaknesses. It presents an opportunity to establish a rapport between the assessor and the adult being assessed, thus helping to alleviate any anxiety about the assessment.

Observations of the learner's use of language and expression can also inform the diagnosis; for example, word retrieval problems or difficulties pronouncing polysyllabic words may be evident.

The following is a guide to the use of the interview pro forma.

Current information

Ask the learner to write her name and address and observe writing style and any difficulties.

Ask about previous courses to determine whether the learner has been making efforts for some years to develop written language proficiency.

Ask about educational aims to get a picture of the learner's goals so the results of the diagnosis can be discussed in light of these.

Ask about the learner's and teachers' attitudes – i.e. how do they perceive the problem? What sort of comments do teachers make or have they made in the past? This often reveals labelling which the learner has internalised, e.g. 'I was lazy/I didn't try hard enough', when in fact she may have put in a great deal of effort.

Schooling

Early problems with reading and/or spelling often indicate the long-term nature and persistence of problems. Some learners started off reading all right, but fell behind at a later stage. Whether or not they had extra help and whether it *did* in fact help can point to the need for *different* strategies and *specialist* help related to specific difficulties (which they may not have received).

Background/history

Establish the history of the learner's language learning:

- **What other factors could explain current problems?**
- **If the learner is bilingual or multilingual, were there any problems in the first language? Was the learner literate in the first language, and to what level?**

There are a number of factors for those who speak English as an additional language which may affect the diagnosis. It is extremely important that these are taken into account if a diagnostic assessment is to be accurate. Please see the guidance and the diagnostic interview form in *Dyslexia and the Bilingual Learner* (see Resources).

Experience with adults often reveals that there may well be other factors in the learner's background to which her difficulties have always been ascribed, such as ill health or disrupted schooling, and to which the learner too has always ascribed them. It is important to explore these with the learner; however, this does not mean that language processing difficulties are not *also* present. Underachievement can sometimes be due to unidentified dyslexic difficulties which have been partially masked and exacerbated by other problems.

Establish any physical impairment of eyes, ears, speech, language or motor coordination, now or as a child. Look for:

- **glue ear or frequent ear infections or colds from ages 3 to 7**
- **'lazy eye' or squint, or history of eye-patching**

- speech problems or 'late talker'
- problems learning to tie shoelaces or catching a ball, or general 'clumsiness'.

A history of any of these can suggest the establishment of confused or inefficient perceptual or motor processing even if the physical problem no longer exists.

Research shows that dyslexia is hereditary so often members of the family have similar difficulties with reading, spelling, memorising, etc. though they may not know they are dyslexic.

Other signs can be an at-risk or difficult birth, or a history of respiratory or neurological problems.

Language/listening behaviours

Establish *undue* difficulty with auditory or auditory-motor processing skills, i.e. general difficulty taking in auditory information.

Word *retrieval* is important; slowness in 'naming' or 'finding' words is a common factor among many dyslexic people. They will often use many words to describe something because they cannot retrieve the 'right' word.

Give examples of multisyllabic words to pronounce, e.g. preliminary, anemone, contemporaneous.*

Phonological processing difficulties are difficulties in segmenting sounds. They are a major indicator of dyslexia. They can be best tested in adults by a 'spoonerism' task where initial sounds are transposed; for example, 'car park' becomes 'par cark'. There is one given in Appendix VII.

When giving adults additional tasks such as spoonerisms, it is helpful to observe them and ask how they did these in order to gain insights into strategies they use.

---

* from the Bangor Dyslexia Text (see Resources)

Learner's description of reading

First identify the learner's reading level by finding out what she reads, e.g. newspapers – which ones and which bits, magazines, stories, novels, course- or work-related texts. Does she read a lot or very little? Why?

Look beneath the reasons given; for example if she tells you she finds reading 'boring', is this because she has to struggle to work out words or because she can't make sense of what she reads?

Try to get a sense from the learner's experience of reading whether any difficulty is one of comprehension, slowness, tracking the print, visual stress or recognising words, which may indicate a visual processing difficulty; or whether it is more a problem of poor decoding or phonetic attack, which may suggest auditory processing difficulties. It is also useful to explore learners' approaches to reading, e.g. do they need dim light or a quiet place, but also, do they try to sound out words or do they guess from context?

If there is a problem with blurry or 'dancing' print, try out a selection of coloured acetate overlays to see if any stabilise the print for her. If so, try to arrange a referral for an assessment of 'scotopic sensitivity' (also known as Meares-Irlen Syndrome – see Resources).

Learner's description of spelling and writing problems

Again, try to determine the appropriate level of writing and spelling; often in dyslexic adults there is a considerable discrepancy between reading level and spelling level. Try to get a sense of the learner's experience of writing and understanding of the writing process. Most dyslexic learners experience great difficulty getting ideas on to paper, finding the 'right' words and organising their ideas.

Inconsistency is an important clue (like electrical impulses which sometimes connect and sometimes do not).

Inability to proof-read can suggest a poor visual memory of a word against which to match an attempt.

Try to find out also how the learner approaches spelling and what strategies, if any, she uses to remember spellings.

Maths

This is included to give a full picture; some dyslexic learners are good at maths, others have difficulty with memorising tables or formulae, transposing figures, arithmetic inaccuracies. They may have especial difficulties with aspects of maths which require many steps or place a heavy load on the short-term memory, e.g. long division or algebra. Some do impressive and creative calculations to compensate for a poor memory for number facts. Others may be dyscalculic, i.e. have significant problems with numerical calculation.

Memory difficulties

Memorisation difficulties particularly relate to sequences, such as the alphabet and months of the year; learners may have had trouble in the past, or still have problems. Often, if they have learned the alphabet they cannot tell where a letter is in the sequence without going back to the beginning. Look to see if they are particularly dependent on meaning and cannot learn by rote.

Sometimes learners are not fully aware of their memorisational difficulties or difficulties with sequence, so in such a case it can be useful to ask them to show you; for example to recite the alphabet or months of the year (particularly the months of the year backward), to ask what letter comes after 'n', to recite the seven times table or to do a digit span test (see Resources). To be accurate, a digit span test needs to be carefully given, following directions (e.g. recited aloud to the learner at one digit per second).

It also helps to find out what techniques they do use if they want to remember something (e.g. something for their course) – is it more visual, auditory, motor? They may also use more 'right brain' strategies, such as imagery or rhythm. Assess if they seem to have to work particularly hard at this. Storing, retrieving and coordinating facts and information are usually problematic.

Learners may be pleased to have achieved success in some of these areas: look for whether they had *undue* difficulty in doing so.

Spatial/temporal

This section contains specific cues to get learners to reflect on the nature of any spatial and/or temporal difficulties. These are used to corroborate other findings. Learners may give their own examples which it is helpful to note verbatim.

Difficulty following directions can indicate short-term auditory memory problems and difficulties with sequences. It may be useful to give a hypothetical example. Giving the learner instructions such as 'point to my right ear with your left hand' can sometimes reveal difficulties with left and right.

Difficulty learning to tell the time may indicate a temporal problem or may be a directional one of transposing the clock face. Some adults find they still have these difficulties and can only use a digital watch.

It is helpful to ask for other examples, e.g. mixing up bus numbers (*36* for *63* or *19* for *16*).

Even if a learner has mastered such tasks now, look for indications of whether it was a struggle to do so.

Dyslexic people may have other difficulties with time, such as estimating time.

Visual-motor

Look for evidence of motor coordination problems. These may be very fine motor coordination problems, sometimes only exhibited in written language. Also, note any description by the learner which suggests confused motor control or lack of motor integration, e.g. the learner intends to write one word but finds her hand writing another, her 'hand adds or writes letters with a mind of its own', her hand tires easily, the learner has to press hard to control the pen or think about forming the letters. Also, observe the way the learner holds the pen and paper while writing, to note any extreme degree of rotation or peculiarity of pen grip.

Note: Suggestions for additional tasks can be found in *Dyslexia and the Bilingual Learner.* Also see the video, *Identifying Dyslexia: a diagnostic interview,* with accompanying notes (see Resources for both).

DYSLEXIA

Diagnostic Interview

Learner's name: .... Date: ....

Address: ....

....

....

Telephone: .... Age (if relevant): ....

College/institution: ....

Contact: ....

Course/work information: ....

Considerations requested:

☐ examinations   ☐ extra time

☐ sympathetic consideration   ☐ extra time in assignments

☐ other (specify)

Other college/educational experiences since leaving school: ....

....

Educational aims of learner: ....

....

Attitude of teachers: ....

....

Attitude of learner/self-assessment of difficulties: ....

....

Schooling – primary

☐ problems learning to read   ☐ received extra help

☐ second language interference   ☐ disruptions/missed school

Comments: ....

Schooling – secondary

☐ problems recognised by school   ☐ exams passed/grades

☐ extra help   ☐ consideration given

☐ exams attempted (particularly English)

Comments: ....

Background/history

☐ ear infections/'glue ear' (primary school)

☐ speech or language difficulties/ 'late talker'

☐ vision problems: squint/lazy eye/ other

☐ other members of family have similar difficulties

☐ motor coordination problems, e.g. tying shoelaces/catching a ball or 'clumsy child' syndrome

☐ any serious health problems, e.g. respiratory, neurological

Comments: ....

Language/listening behaviours

☐ trouble listening   ☐ word retrieval problems

☐ trouble concentrating with background noise

☐ problems with listening and taking notes simultaneously

☐ pronunciation difficulties, especially with multisyllabic words

☐ phonological processing problems, e.g. with spoonerisms

Comments: ....

Reading

Approximate level:

☐ needs to reread frequently   ☐ oral reading difficulties

☐ comprehension difficulties   ☐ problems tracking print

☐ word recognition problems   ☐ print 'dances', blurs or irritates eyes

☐ decoding problems

Approaches used by learner:

Comments: ....

Writing and spelling

Approximate level:

- ☐ difficulty getting ideas down on paper
- ☐ word retrieval problems
- ☐ problems with grammar/sentence structure/punctuation
- ☐ problems with organisation and planning

Planning strategies used:

- ☐ 'good' days and 'bad' days
- ☐ difficulties remembering what words look like
- ☐ difficulties discriminating 'holding' sounds
- ☐ difficulties 'seeing' errors/proof-reading

General spelling approaches used by learner:

Comments: ....

Maths

- ☐ difficulties memorising times tables
- ☐ difficulties memorising basic number facts
- ☐ other (specify)
- ☐ difficulties with long division/ algebra, etc.
- ☐ general proficiency

General approach:

Comments: ....

Memory difficulties

- ☐ alphabet
- ☐ months/days/seasons
- ☐ telephone numbers
- ☐ other (specify)
- ☐ erratic memory
- ☐ names, dates, factual information
- ☐ difficulties remembering verbal directions or instructions

Strategies used:

Comments: ....

Spatial/temporal

- [ ] difficulties learning to tell time
- [ ] left/right confusions
- [ ] other (specify)

- [ ] map reading difficulties
- [ ] gets lost easily

Comments: ....

Visual-motor

- [ ] copying difficulties

- [ ] letter reversals

- [ ] unusual paper position

- [ ] unusual pen grip

- [ ] left-handed

- [ ] difficulties controlling pen

- [ ] irregular or awkward letter construction

- [ ] problems with writing what's intended/much crossing out, etc.

- [ ] hand gets tired after short period of writing

Other information:

3 | Reading

The second stage of the diagnostic assessment after the interview is to analyse the learner's reading through a miscue analysis of oral reading, followed by the learner's retelling of the passage and specific comprehension questions. Non-word and single-word reading tasks should also be given to the learner to read in order to inform the analysis. (These are included in the appendices.)

The aim of the analysis is to determine the nature and extent of the learner's difficulties with reading. However, in order to do this, it is important that the assessor is clear about the nature of the reading process and the way in which proficient readers read. As Beech and Singleton (1997) point out, there is still much theoretical speculation about reading but 'a consensus is comparatively all too infrequent.' Assumptions can influence the tutor's perception of the reader's difficulties. For example, a learner who relies heavily on context to work out words but has good comprehension may be perceived as having no reading problems. On closer look, however, such a learner may be struggling with unfamiliar words, and may be unable to tackle words out of context. *Having* to rely on context is a handicap, not a sign of a competent reader; the latter can rapidly read single words in any context, even the most unexpected.

On the other hand, readers may read a passage with little or no apparent difficulty and again be perceived as having no reading problems. Whereas, if comprehension is then tested, some learners may be seen to have understood little of what they read.

For a full discussion of the reading process and how dyslexia may affect readers, see 'The Reading Process' (Appendix I). Also refer to Ellis, 1993, Marilyn Adams, 1990 and Jackson and Coltheart, 2001.

SELECTING A READING PASSAGE

It is necessary to select a passage at the right level in order both to generate enough errors and to assess learners' reading skills in relation to the demands of their jobs or courses.

Through the interview, the tutor should find out what sort of reading the learner does, both for pleasure and for work or study, in order to try to assess the learner's level. The passage selected should be unfamiliar and the learner should not be able to use prior knowledge to answer comprehension questions on it. It should be long and complex enough to reveal any comprehension problems. It is important that vocabulary in the passage is not repetitive, but is varied. The passage should also be difficult enough to reveal the learner's strategies for dealing with unknown words and accessing and monitoring meaning.

It can be useful to do a readability analysis of the passage using Fogg or Smog or any similar method. The Fogg readability formula is included here (Appendix II). There are many criticisms of readability methods but they can be helpful as a guide to the level of reading material. It is important, however, to remember that these are formulas for readability so the 'reading age' from such an analysis is a guide *only* to the difficulty of the passage and does *not* give a reading age for the learner.

One of the problems with assessing the reading of a more advanced learner is that the learner's difficulties may not show up with a passage which is relatively easy, whereas significant problems may occur with a more difficult passage. If learners are struggling with the reading on a course, it is important to identify the kind of problems they will encounter in their course of study.

However, the passage should not be so difficult for the learner that she cannot recognise or work out enough words to make sense of the passage; if the struggle seems too great, or there are too many miscues, try an easier passage! This book contains a selection of reading passages at different levels which may be used or may act as examples regarding length and level of difficulty for choosing your own. See also *Dyslexia and the Bilingual Learner* for passages which avoid idiomatic language and unfamiliar cultural contexts for those speaking English as an additional language.

MISCUE ANALYSIS

Miscue analysis is a tool for looking closely at the types of strategies a reader uses as she reads. It was devised by an American educationalist, Kenneth Goodman, and is based upon psycholinguistic theory. Its aim is to observe how well the reader processes visual material in the search for meaning and how fluent, regardless of the reading level, her reading is.

'Goodman coined the word "miscue" in the 1960s to describe any departure the reader makes from the actual words of the text. . . Goodman's purpose in coining this term "miscue" was twofold – First, he wanted to get away from the notion that every departure from the words of the text is necessarily bad, something to be considered an error. Second, he wanted to emphasize how such departures from the text indicated which language cue systems the reader is using and not using, at least at the particular moment; the pattern of miscues thus suggests the reader's strengths as well as weaknesses . . .' (Weaver, 1988)

The aim of miscue analysis is to examine miscues 'from a point of view of how close they are to what had been expected' in order to identify 'the pattern of a reader's strengths and weaknesses. These patterns may reveal linguistic or conceptual weaknesses' . . . or may show how a reader who 'repeats words and phrases, miscues and corrects, is deeply and actively processing printed material for meaning.' (*The Aims of Miscue Analysis*, source unknown.) Used carefully, it remains a very useful tool for identifying a reader's strengths and weaknesses in processing written language.

The cueing systems

There are three major cueing systems which the reader can use in reading a text.

Grapho/phonic cues: *letter/sound* cues, i.e. visual analysis of letter patterns/the correspondences between letters (graphemes) and sounds (phonemes).

Semantic cues: *meaning* cues from each sentence, both forward and backward, and from the whole as the reader progresses.

Syntactic cues: *grammatical* cues including word order, grammatical endings, function words and sentence structure.

1. The grapho/phonic system

The grapho/phonic system may be seen as two sub-systems: one of visual whole-word recognition or analysis of visual patterns and the other of the correspondence between letters and sounds. Although Goodman, Frank Smith and others in the 1960s and 1970s put forward the theory that the skilled reader uses a minimum of visual cues, only enough to *predict* a word, more recent research and theory suggests that the skilled reader reads *primarily* from rapid word recognition based on rapid visual analysis with reference to an internal lexicon. The phonic or 'sounding out' route is used by the skilled reader primarily when confronted with an unfamiliar word.

The learner reader may go through a phase of relying on the phonic route to 'crack the code' but by the reading age of eight, receptiveness to visual cues is dominating the reading process (Marie Clay, 1985). Automaticity in reading depends on acquiring rapid word recognition without reliance on processing the sounds. Over-reliance on the phonic route may suggest difficulties in recognising familiar words. If the learner is not monitoring for meaning and is making nonsense or non-word miscues, then she is over-relying on the grapho/phonic system.

On the other hand, if the miscues show poor visual or phonic resemblance, then the learner may have a weakness in the grapho/phonic system. They may have difficulties with segmenting and manipulating sounds or in associating sounds with letters. Often the learner is able to use initial letters but shows a weakness in decoding or recognising endings or middles. Such learners will often have to compensate by relying more on semantic and syntactic cues.

2. The semantic system

This system provides information about the appropriateness of meaning given by the context of a word. For example, the sentence, 'They refurnished their house' read as, 'They refurnished their home', would show that the reader has kept the meaning largely intact. However, the sentence read as, 'They refurnished their horse', shows a weakness in the use of the semantic system. The skilled reader monitors for meaning both reading ahead and reading back. For example in the following sentences, 'She wanted to sell her house. She hoped someone would be happy living in it,' a substitution of 'horse' for 'house' makes sense for the first sentence but not when you add the second. A reader who makes such miscues is not reading ahead to monitor meaning.

3. The syntactic system

This system provides information about grammatical appropriateness. Language is rule-governed and intuitive knowledge of grammatical structures and conventions is part of knowing a language. Grammatical structures limit the possible choices a reader can make.

Examples of poor use of this system would be reading the sentence, 'She is going to show us where the shop is' as 'She is *go* to show us where the shop is', 'She is going to *showed* us where the shop is' or 'She is going to show us *were* the shop is'.

Readers who speak English as an additional language or a variety of English other than Standard English may not be able to use this system fully. On the other hand, they may adapt what they read to their 'own' grammar. For instance, a learner from some parts of London might read, 'We were all at the pub last night' as 'We *was* all at the pub last night'. This adapting of grammar or vocabulary is part of what a skilled reader does in getting meaning from a text and does *not* show poor use of the syntactic system.

Procedure

Miscue analysis is not a *test* but a way of obtaining an overall picture of the learner's strengths and weaknesses in reading. It should be shared with the learner so that she fully understands its purpose and how it can lead to more effective strategies for learning and teaching by identifying her strengths and weaknesses.

Select a passage for the learner to read aloud. It should be slightly above the learner's reading level, of moderate difficulty. It should generate at least 20 to 30 miscues, depending on the level and length of the passage, to reveal a pattern of difficulty. If there are too many more you may not get a true picture of their comprehension. Photocopy the passage for yourself to mark up and enlarge it so the font is 12 point for GCSE level and 14 point for lower levels. It is important to tape the learner reading so that you can mark up the passage later and can concentrate on observing the reader; with experience you may not need to use a tape, but it is generally advisable because you may want to listen more than once.

Explain to the learner why you need to hear her read aloud, so that you can see how she reads and what kind of difficulties she is having.

Suggest that the learner look over the passage first and begin reading when ready. Tell the learner to read for meaning as you will ask her to tell you about what she read. Tell her not to worry about difficulties and to feel free to pause, read bits over and make guesses, but that you will not help because you want to see how she works the words out herself.

After the learner has finished reading, remove the text and ask her to tell you what it was about in as much detail as she can remember. Record this *verbatim*. Follow with some questions about significant details from the passage.

If the learner is an advanced reader, she may not make enough errors, even when you try a more difficult text. In this case an analysis of comprehension and reading style may be adequate to identify the learner's strengths and weaknesses if used in conjunction with single word reading of regular and irregular words and non-words.

Marking system

Errors can be recorded in different ways, but the following chart includes the most useful symbols. (Chart adapted from M. Walsh, June 1979.)

Miscue	Symbol	
Non-response	work ----------	Use a broken line to indicate an inability or refusal to attempt a word.
Substitution appropriate	*play* work	Write substituted word above appropriate part of text.
Insertion	*his* for ⌃ work	Indicate by insertion sign, and write inserted word above.
Omission	(work)	Circle word, words or parts of words omitted.
Repetition	work	Underline words repeated.
Correction	*play* © work	Place a small © beside corrected word ⓂⒸ for miscorrection
Reversal	work ⟩hard o ＼ n	Symbol that shows which parts of letters, words, phrases, or clauses have been interchanged.
Hesitation	work / hard	Hesitation between two words.
	work // hard	Extra long hesitation.

It is also useful to use Ⓥ for language variety for a miscue which is the result of the reader using non-Standard English grammar.

In recording non-word substitutions, spelling should reflect grapho/phonic cues that the reader is using. For example, if a reader reads *phenomena* as fu-hon-ma, it should be spelled above the original as *phuhonma* to show that the reader is using the 'ph' as a cue.

You should note repetitions and self-corrections as these are signs of monitoring meaning. You should also note hesitations and other aspects of reading style (see 'Reading Style Analysis' in this chapter).

Analysing miscues

The following coding system is adapted from Goodman and has been modified to aid accurate assessment of reading difficulties.

> We code   (+) for effective use of a cueing system
>
>   (✓) for partial use of a cueing system
>
>   (o) for little or no use of a cueing system
>
> *Each error is coded for all three cueing systems.*

1. The grapho/phonic system

How much does the miscue *look* like what was expected?
How much does the miscue *sound* like what was expected?

In most adult readers, beyond the basic literacy stage, the look of a word should predominate and for advanced readers the need to rely on the phonic aspect should be minimal. However, we code both columns to help observe if the learner is using the immediate visual route or the mediated phonic route. In most cases the coding of these will be similar or the stronger system will be revealed by close analysis.

For example: *heard* for *head* would show a (+) for the graphic or visual cue but a (✓) for the phonic or sounding out, showing the reader relying on visual whole word recognition.

On the other hand: *fackade* for *facade* would show a (+) for the phonic and a (✓) for the visual system because it is a non-word (see below). Here the reader is relying on 'sounding out' rather than visual recognition.

Grapho/phonic similarity is high (+) if most of the word (beginning, middle and end) has a high graphic similarity and/or has been decoded with a fair amount of accuracy. To identify high graphic similarity it is useful to observe your own miscues when you read, as a rule of thumb.

Non-word substitutions tend to show an over-reliance on phonic cues. As the visual system relies on whole-word as well as letter and part-word recognition, it is helpful *not* to code these as (+) in the visual column, even when they are very similar graphically, such as *foritude* for *fortitude*. In this case, it should be coded (✓).

Grapho/phonic similarity is partial (✓) if the miscue has some graphic similarity and/or some part or parts of the word have been accurately decoded.

If there is little or no similarity or accurate decoding, then the reader shows no grapho/phonic strength (o).

Some examples of miscue with high grapho/phonic similarity:

Text	Miscue	Visual	Phonic
waist	wrist	+	✓
straightened	strengthened	+	✓
owing	owning	+	✓
promptings	promotings	+	✓
acclimatisation	acclimatation	✓	+
detriment	determent	✓	+

Examples of miscues with partial grapho/phonic similarity:

Text	Miscue	Visual	Phonic
present	patient	✓	✓
fortitude	fortunate	✓	✓
sedately	sadly	✓	✓
acclimatisation	accumulation	✓	✓
opposite	ossopit	✓	✓

Examples of miscues with little or no grapho/phonic similarity:

Text	Miscue	Visual	Phonic
present	perched	o	o
almost	awfully	o	o
aghast	gasingly	o	o
usual	surface	o	o
flickering	blinking	o	o

Omissions and insertions demonstrate no use of grapho/phonic cues and may be coded with a dash (–) in the grapho/phonic columns.

2. The semantic system

Is the miscue acceptable in relation to the meaning that the context gives a word? Semantic strength is high when the *original meaning* of the sentence is relatively unchanged. Most miscues will modify the meaning to some extent, but they are highly acceptable (+) when they are close to the author's intent within the context of the whole passage.

Semantic strength is partial (✓) when the miscue is appropriate within a single sentence but not within the total context, as in the example of horse/house given earlier.

If there is no evidence of semantic acceptability, the miscue is coded as (o).

It is advisable to code semantic miscues either (+) or (o) as much as possible, and to use the (✓) sparingly. This, in conjunction with the number of corrections that the reader makes, will give a much clearer picture of how well the reader is actually reading for meaning.

Some examples of miscues with high semantic acceptability (+):

Text	Miscue
violent *(explosions)*	volcanic
disruptive *(adolescent)*	destructive
(lit my) smoke	cigarette
(seemed to) afford	offer
(him much pleasure)	

An example of partial semantic acceptability (✓):

Text	Miscue
(We carried just about everything, animals, *whiskey),* dynamite	diamonds

(The next sentence goes on to say, 'There were times when I felt I was flying a bomb.')

Examples of poor semantic acceptability (o):

Text	Miscue
(Up on the roof the) pigeons *(were gathered)*	pigments
(his) owner	over
(sent him to London Zoo as a) present	parent
He *(arrived in the back of a small van)*	we

Non-words are always coded (o).

3. The syntactic system

Does the miscue work grammatically in the context of the sentence? Miscues are syntactically either appropriate (+) or not appropriate (o), so there is no partial strength.

Examples of miscues which show syntactic strength (+):

Text	Miscue
(send him as a) present	patient
(he had huge) arms	hands
(If he had) straightened *(up)*	stretched
fully (mature)	finally

To be coded as a (+), a miscue must be a real word.

Examples which show syntactic weakness (o):

Text	Miscue
(was quite) devoid *(of hair)*	devote
(both) sides *(of his face)*	besides
(wandered about) aimlessly	airless
(a) glitter *(of ironic laughter)*	greater

Language variety (v) miscues which are appropriate to the learner's spoken grammar should be coded as (+). For example, a Caribbean Creole speaker might read:

like Ⓥ

'Just about everybody likes to dance.'

As long as it is grammatically correct, the sentence does not need to make sense in order to be coded (+).

However, semantic miscue can only be a (+) if it is also grammatically (+).

Non-word substitutions are always coded (o) both semantically and syntactically.

Insertions and omissions should be coded to show syntactic and semantic strengths and weaknesses.

For example:

'For the first time in my life I was (really) scared…'

and:

'I was never quite sure whether $\overset{the}{\wedge}$ telegraph poles were very strong…'

Both show semantic and syntactic acceptability; whereas:

'Sometimes he left (after) a few days…'

changes the meaning and is syntactically weak.

It is helpful to code two words together if one of the words has been adjusted to affect the other; for example, (I kicked the door frame) *and discovered . . .*' for *to discover*, but to code them separately otherwise.

Corrections

Corrections should be noted in the final column with a tick or some other mark. They indicate that the reader is monitoring meaning and should be considered as part of the reader's reading style. You should also note miscorrections.

Final points

- You are looking for an *overall pattern*.

- This is a *tool for observation* – you need to get experience of using it and it won't give you all the answers.

- Readers may be *inconsistent* in using cueing systems.

- You need to interpret the miscue analysis in the light of the reader's comprehension. Check *comprehension* orally, through asking the learner:

  - to tell you in as much detail as possible what she remembers, to show spontaneous recall and sequencing

  - questions which show ability to make inferences from the text as well as give literal answers.

- It is very important to observe *reading style* (e.g. word for word, jerky, ignoring punctuation or lots of hesitations and repetitions, etc).

Readers with primarily *(visual)* word recognition problems often rely on a phonic approach and will make non-word substitutions, frequently showing semantic weaknesses. They often ignore punctuation, read jerkily and may miss out words or lose their place. They also show few signs of monitoring comprehension (e.g. repetitions and corrections) and their comprehension is frequently vague because all their concentration is going into trying to recognise or work out the words.

Readers with mainly poor auditory *(or phonological)* skills will be unsuccessful or only partly successful in using a phonic approach. They may read with good understanding but will often struggle to decode words they don't know, rely heavily on context and substitute whole words that show attempts to make sense of the passage. They usually make frequent repetitions and often self-correct. In spite of their difficulties, their comprehension is frequently good (if the text does not contain too many new words) with spontaneous recall of significant details.

References

Adams, M.J., *Beginning to Read*, MIT Press, 1990.

The Aims of Miscue Analysis (source unknown).

Beech and Singleton (eds.), *The Psychological Assessment of Reading*, Routledge, 1997.

Ellis, A., *Reading, Writing and Dyslexia*, 2nd edition, Lawrence Erlbaum Associates, 1993.

Goodman, Y. and Burke, C., *Reading Miscue Inventory Manual Procedure for Diagnosis and Evaluation*, New York: Macmillan, 1972.

Jackson, N.E. and Coltheart, M., *Routes to Reading Success and Failure*, USA: Psychology Press, 2001.

Walsh, M., 'Miscue Analysis', ALU Newsletter , No. 5, June 1979.

Snowling, M., 'From language to reading and dyslexia', *Dyslexia*, Vol. 7, No. 1, 2001.

Weaver, C., *Reading Process and Practice*, Heinemann, 1988.

CHUMLEY

Chumley was a full-grown//chimpanzee. his owner, a District Officer, was/finding the ape's large size rather awkward, and he wanted to send him to London Zoo as a /present, so that he could visit the animals when he was back in England on leave. He wrote asking us if we would mind taking Chumley back with us when we left, and/depositing him at his new home in London, and we replied that we would not mind at all.

He arrived in the/back of a small van, seated sedately in a huge crate. when the doors of his crate were opened and Chumley stepped out with all the ease and self-confidence of a film star, I was considerably shaken, for, standing on his//bow legs in a normal slouching chimp position, he came up to my//waist, and if he had straightened up, his head would have been on a level with my chest. He had huge arms, and must have//measured at least twice my/measurements round his //hairy chest. Owing to bad tooth growth both sides of his face were swollen out of all proportion, and this gave him a /weird /pugilistic look. His eyes were small, deep-set and // intelligent the top of his head was nearly bald//owing, I discovered later, to his habit of sitting and rubbing the palms of his hand backwards across his head, an exercise which seemed to afford him much pleasure and which he persisted in until the top of his skull/was quite devoid of hair. This was no young chimp as I had expected, but a//veteran of about eight or nine years, fully mature, strong as a powerful.

Miscue Analysis Form

Date: ....

Learner's name: ...... *Peter* ...... Reading selection: ...... *Chumley* ......

Script	Miscue	Grapho/phonic		Semantic	Syntactic	Corrections
		Visual	Phonetic			
Chumley	Cherrylyn	✓	o	+	+	✓
District	Director	✓	o	✓	o	✓
apes	open	✓	o	o	o	✓
present	parent	+	✓	o	+	
wrote	wote	✓	✓	o	o	✓
we	he	✓	o	o	+	
his	the	o	o	+	+	✓
the	a	o	o	o	+	✓
seated	standing	o	o	✓	+	
„	sitting	✓	✓	+	+	✓
sedately	steadily	✓	o	+	+	
crate	cage	✓	o	+	+	
his	the	o	o	+	+	✓
chumley	cherrily	✓	✓	+	+	
film	fully	✓	o	o	o	✓
slouching	secluding	✓	o	o	o	
straightened	strengthened	+	✓	o	o	✓
„	stretched	✓	✓	+	+	(mc)
head	hand	✓	✓	o	+	
measured	muscles	✓	o	o	o	
tooth	toes	✓	o	o	o	✓
this	his	✓	o	o	o	✓
weird	warid	✓	✓	o	o	
pugilistic	puglistic	✓	+	o	o	
persisted	persided	✓	✓	o	o	✓
skull	skin	✓	✓	o	+	
devoid	divided	✓	✓	o	o	
fully	finally	✓	✓	o	+	
as	and	✓	o	o	o	

Observations from reading:

No. of repetitions ...... *14* ......

No. of corrections ...... *13* ......

Observed strengths/weaknesses:

Reading style (see attached sheet):

Frequent repetitions and corrections show he is monitoring meaning. Often hesitates before difficult words/when unsure of meaning shows excellent and detailed memory of passage but his struggle with decoding words makes reading arduous. Weaknesses in grapho/phonic system, particularly in using phonic cues. Usually substitutes whole words but does not predict, but high numbers of corrections and repetitions shows he relies heavily on context: needs to use context better to predict and to improve sight vocabulary.

Miscue Analysis Form

Date: ....

Learner's name: .... Reading selection: ....

Script	Miscue	Grapho/phonic		Semantic	Syntactic	Corrections
		Visual	Phonetic			

Observations from reading: Reading style (see attached sheet):

No. of repetitions ....

No. of corrections ....

Observed strengths/weaknesses:

READING STYLE ANALYSIS

When analysing a learner's reading, it is important to consider the learner's reading style as a whole and in its various aspects, as well as the learner's comprehension as part of a miscue analysis. The aim is to draw up a profile of the reader in terms of the approach to reading, strategies used, strengths and weaknesses. It is this whole picture that enables an accurate analysis which can be the basis of a clear understanding of the learner's difficulties and the setting up of an effective individual learning programme.

The following is a guide for drawing up such a reading profile.

Overall style

Does the learner read:

- **word-for-word?**
- **without regard for punctuation?**
- **jerkily?**
- **fluently with hesitations only before difficult words?**
- **stressing each syllable, even pitch, heavy stress?**
- **pausing after phrases and whole sentences at punctuation points?**

What do these tell you about the learner's reading approach and difficulties?

Reading speed is also important to observe. If a learner is reading particularly slowly, this will be important for any course work, exams or job-related reading they are expected to do. The average (silent) reading speed for an adult is 200–400 words per minute. You may want to give an additional silent reading passage to check reading speed.

Hesitations

Does the reader make frequent or long hesitations before words or before bits of words? Hesitations show where the reader has a problem – is it before unexpected words, words which the reader doesn't recognise, or words the reader can't 'attack' or sound out?

Repetitions

Does the reader repeat words/phrases/whole sentences? Frequent repetitions show the reader is searching for and consolidating meaning. Look at repetitions in conjunction with the number of corrections, and semantic codings and their overall comprehension.

Visual-motor tracking

Does the reader lose place easily, miss out words or lines, need to use a finger for tracking?

Are there examples of sequential errors? Interference of words from one line of print to the one above or below?

Corrections

Does the reader correct miscues – often, occasionally, never?

Does the reader seem to be monitoring meaning by self-correcting?

Does the reader overcorrect, e.g. errors which do not impede or alter meaning?

Does the reader miscorrect accurate reading?

Cueing systems

What kind of cueing systems does the reader seem to be using for unfamiliar words?

- **Syllables and letter clusters**
- **Little words in bigger words**
- **Visual analysis by analogy**
- **Syntactic cues and semantic content, e.g. prediction**

Does the reader seem to have limited word attack skills?

Does the reader have only one way of attacking unfamiliar words, e.g. lack flexibility or the ability to use a variety of cueing systems?

Does the reader:

- **misread common/familiar words?**
- **have to rely on 'sounding-out' because of failure to recognise familiar words?**

Insertions, omissions and refusals

Insertions and omissions will indicate different things depending on whether or not they retain the meaning and syntax. Skilled readers will sometimes omit or insert small words which do not affect the meaning or grammar, but omissions or insertions which lose the sense will often indicate visual processing difficulties.

Refusals differ from omissions in that omissions are unintentional whereas refusals usually indicate that the reader does not know the word and is unable to use a phonic approach to guess at it.

COMPREHENSION

Retelling

Was the reader able to extract main points and significant details from the text?

How does the reader relate details?

- **in the order they were given?**
- **in any kind of developmental order?**
- **at random?**

Are there signs of sequential or organisational difficulties?

Can the reader see inherent connections between details? Draw conclusions? Are problems with short-term or 'working' memory interfering with complex comprehension skills?

Specific questions

Do the reader's answers confirm retelling: are there contradictions?

Is the reader able to add/focus on details which may have been omitted in the retelling?

Do her answers confirm comprehension of particular points/ability to draw conclusions or make inferences?

Language and vocabulary

Does the reader reveal expressive language difficulties, e.g.

- **word retrieval problems**
- **vocabulary confusions**
- **problems saying what she means/vague use of language?**

Was the vocabulary difficult or unfamiliar? (note examples)

Is the reader familiar with/does she know the meaning of words she doesn't recognise in print?

Try to put together all your observations into a description of how the reader reads. What does this tell you about underlying processing and cognitive (e.g. memory) strengths and weaknesses?

SINGLE WORD AND NON-WORD TESTING

It is important to look at single word and non-word reading to see how the reader functions without the support of context. Results from these help identify, clarify or confirm difficulties identified through the miscue analysis.

When giving these tests, in addition to scoring, record the reader's attempt at each word if it is not correct, in order to help identify the difficulties and strategies the reader is using. You may also find it helpful to ask the reader how she is approaching the task.

Three types of 'tests' are included in Appendix IV: two Irregular Word Lists, one for more advanced and one for less advanced readers, the Long Regular Word List and the Snowling Graded Non-word Reading Test (revised pilot version).

The Irregular Word Lists are made up of irregular words, i.e. those which cannot be pronounced accurately by using basic phonic 'rules'. Instead, they need to be *recognised* in order to read them accurately. Such words are useful in helping to determine a reader's visual recognition skills.

However, because these words do rely on recognition for accurate reading, the reader must *know* the words in print in order to read them. Such a task is only reliable as a guide to the reader's difficulties when using words which are familiar to the reader. Therefore, the lists should be used as a resource to select words appropriate to each particular learner. *It is a reader's difficulty in recognising familiar words that you are looking for.*

The Long Regular Word List, on the other hand, is composed of words which can be accurately 'read' by using phonic 'rules' whether the reader knows them or not, or indeed has any idea of their meaning at all. Such words can indicate the reader's ability to use a phonic strategy and also to 'track' long words. Therefore, this list should be given in its entirety (unless the reader cannot attempt them or has great difficulty in reading them). It is useful to compare the reader's performance on the irregular and regular words; often the reader is much better at one than the other. This can then inform the analysis of the learner's strengths and weaknesses in reading.

However, as the long regular words are indeed *words*, a reader can read the familiar ones by recognising them. To get a more accurate picture of the reader's skills in phonic attack, it is particularly useful to give the reader non-words to read as these can *only* be read through phonic attack. The Snowling Graded Non-word Reading Test (revised pilot version) is therefore included for this purpose. The test is not standardised for adults so it can only be used to provide information on the reader's phonic skills. It is worth remembering, however, that a proficient reader will be able to 'read' *all* of these non-words with no difficulty whatsoever; consequently *any* difficulties an adult has may be illuminating and are likely to be significant.

When giving the non-word test, it is best to enlarge the non-words to 16-point at least, and space them out or show them singly. This minimises any visual difficulties and gives a truer picture of phonological difficulties.

Note: If doing a significant amount of diagnostic work with dyslexic learners, I recommend purchasing the published version of the Snowling Graded Non-word Reading Test (see Resources). The non-words are printed individually on cards. It is only normed for ages 5 to 11 years but can be used with all age groups.

4 | Spelling Error Analysis

Spelling error analysis is a way of analysing a learner's spellings in order to identify the learner's strengths and weaknesses and approach to spelling, as part of the diagnostic process.

Many adults who have developed strategies for coping with reading continue to have considerable problems with spelling and writing which seriously affect their academic performance. A large discrepancy between the level of reading and that of spelling is one indicator of possible dyslexia, particularly when the types of errors show *persistent* difficulty in acquiring sounds, letter patterns and/or the conventions of English spelling.

The analysis and categorisation of errors is based on a modification of the work of Margaret Peters.

Introducing the spelling dictation

A piece of the learner's writing which contains at least 20–25 errors is needed in order to identify a pattern of difficulty. A diagnostic dictation at the appropriate level for the learner is more likely to reveal the extent and pattern of the learner's difficulties than a piece of free writing where the learner may avoid words she is unable to spell. Explain to the learner that the dictation is not a test, but that it will help you to identify what kinds of difficulties she has and enable you to suggest the best ways of overcoming them.

Ask the learner to make a best guess if she does not know how to spell some of the words. It may be helpful to explain to the learner the value of guessing, that it can help you both to see exactly where her difficulties lie. If the learner can appreciate the usefulness of errors, she is likely to be less anxious and feel more of a participant in the diagnostic process. Dictate the passage at a pace the learner can easily follow. Tell the learner that you will not put in punctuation but will expect her to do it herself. If the learner has difficulty remembering, slow down or break the sentence into smaller chunks. Also tell the learner she will have time afterwards to proof-read for punctuation and to correct spellings if she wants.

When the dictation is completed, ask the learner to read over what she has written and to underline words she thinks are wrong. This will show you if the learner can 'see' her own errors. The learner may correct words if she thinks she can by writing the correct version above the incorrect attempt, in the margin or at the bottom of the page, but explain that she should not worry if she cannot correct them.

It is very important to observe the learner writing as this will show you how much time she has to spend thinking about spellings, how 'automatic' spelling and handwriting are, and whether she has handwriting problems such as having to press hard to control the pen, adding or omitting letters unintentionally, or having difficulty getting the hand to go in the intended direction (e.g. writing a 'd' for a 'g').

The dictation included here (see Appendix V) is from Margaret Peters and Brigid Smith. The most difficult of theirs are graded for children aged 10–11. More advanced learners may therefore not make enough errors on the dictation and can be given additional words from the advanced spelling list (see Appendix VI) to generate more errors. (For more advanced and vocationally based dictations, see Hulley, 1992.)

Other graded dictations, modelled on those of Margaret Peters, are available in *Dyslexia and the Bilingual Learner* (see Resources). These contain vocabulary, grammatical structures and context which are likely to be more familiar to adult learners of English as an additional language.

Classifying the errors

Check the piece of writing for errors and compare the learner's spelling errors with the correct spellings using the spelling analysis chart.

Errors are classified in the following categories.

A. Logical phonetic alternatives which also follow English spelling convention, i.e. they would be an 'acceptable' alternative. Examples of these errors would be *serface* for *surface*, *groops* for *groups*, *resently* for *recently*. Homonyms also fall into this category. A good rule of thumb is to see if you can think of a word in English which follows the same pattern, e.g. *pearants* is acceptable because *pear* and *wear* have the same *ear* sound. However, *engoy* for *enjoy* is not acceptable because the 'g' is always hard when followed by an 'o'.

B. Visual sequential errors, i.e. usually two letters out of order, as in *Britian* for *Britain*, *claer* for *clear* and *dose* for *does*. These are errors to do with visual rather than auditory memory; significant sounds which are missequenced, such as the 'r' in *hreat* for *heart* would be categorised in Column D.

C. Rule base errors, or those which show lack of awareness of spelling rules or are unacceptable phonetic alternatives. Examples would be *copys* for *copies*, *jocked* for *joked*, *pocet* for *pocket* (because 'c' followed by 'e' would be pronounced *poset*), *stashun* for *station* (because the sound *shun* is not spelled that way as a suffix), *imediatly* for *immediately*.

D. Sounds missing, misheard or missequenced. Sometimes they can be very disordered. Examples are *wising* for *whistling*, *kinf* for *knife*, *scelye* for *scarcely*, *sepate* for *separate*, *volient* for *violent*.

E. Motor errors which may take the form of handwriting errors, repetition or omission of letters, telescoping or perseverating. Telescoping means that repeated letters, or a syllable in a multisyllabic word, have been omitted. Telescoping is visual-motor rather than auditory; that is, the missing letters are not significant sounds within a syllable, but rather repeated or similar looking and sounding letters or whole syllables; it shows a lack of eye-to-hand coordination. Examples of telescoping would be *beging* for *beginning* and *presion* for *precision*.

Perseveration is an inability to stop doing something, such as repeating a pattern. An example of perseveration would be *machinine* for *machine* where the hand repeats a letter pattern.

However, it is not always easy to tell if these sorts of error are motor or auditory; they need to be looked at in the context of the 'pattern' of the writer's errors. Sometimes, observation will give you a good clue. One learner wrote *folling* for *following*; when she tried to correct it, she wrote *folowing*, omitting the second 'l'. It was easy then to see that she had telescoped the word because of visual-motor problems; that is, being unable to keep track of all the letters and syllables as she wrote.

Another type of motor error is when one word is substituted for another, i.e. the hand 'takes over' and writes another word than the one intended, for example *particular* for *peculiar* or *serious* for *series*.

Again, such substitutions are not always motor; a learner with auditory processing weaknesses will sometimes substitute another word because it 'looks right' (i.e. it is a real word) and she is unable to discriminate between similar sounding words. In this case, they would be classified in Column D.

Decide how to classify each error and tick the appropriate column. If a spelling attempt contains two or more errors which are classified differently, tick the column further to the right. This means you are categorising the most severe error, i.e. D and E suggest the most serious problems. Where errors seem difficult to classify, such as those which may be motor or auditory, it may be useful to hold these until the end when you can see the overall pattern of errors. Two learners may spell a word the same way for different reasons. Remember, it is the overall pattern of errors which is important.

Interpretation of the spelling error analysis chart

Learners may make errors of all types, but note the frequency with which errors fall into the different columns. Learners will generally reveal a pattern, with a predominance of errors in one or two columns.

Column A

This column will include words which are near to the correct spelling or seem to be possible 'alternative spellings'. They show the learner is close to learning appropriate combinations of letters and to integrating 'rules' for generalising English spelling patterns.

If most of the errors are in this column, the learner understands English spelling convention and with practice is probably on the way to becoming a successful speller. However, if these sorts of errors persist and the learner continues to make large numbers of errors, she may have a poor visual memory and may need to develop auditory and other strategies for remembering.

Column B

A number of errors in this column indicates the learner has difficulty remembering or re-visualising the sequence of the letters correctly. The visual memory of the word is poor, so other strategies for remembering need to be developed.

Column C

A large number of errors in this column show that the learner does not have a clear idea of which combination of letters to use. She may be making a phonetic attempt, but fails to follow English spelling convention, i.e. the word could not be spelled like that in English. The learner probably has difficulties assimilating rules and generalising; she may need to be taught how words are built up and to link words to those of a similar pattern. Errors in Column C also suggest a weakness in visual memory.

Column D

A larger number of errors here shows difficulty in matching sounds with appropriate letters; a learner with these errors may have difficulty discriminating or segmenting sounds, or 'holding' sounds in short-term auditory memory. The learner will therefore need visual and lexical strategies, such as words within words, for learning.

Column E

Errors in this column may indicate the learner is not able to keep track of the whole word while writing, but may 'get lost' in it, particularly when it is multisyllabic. The learner may have eye-to-hand coordination problems, or handwriting problems such as difficulty controlling the pen.

General comments

If a learner has most errors in Column A, it suggests that she is on the way to understanding English spelling convention. The further to the right the errors are, the more difficulty the learner is likely to have in acquiring spellings. A large number of errors in Column C may indicate that the learner has visual perceptual processing difficulties, with a weak memory for the way words look and problems with making generalisations about language. This is especially likely if she also has errors in Columns A, B and/or E. A learner with a large number of errors in Column D is likely to have auditory processing difficulties. Some learners will have a mixture of difficulties, but it is helpful to identify where the main difficulties lie as this will help in finding effective strategies for learning.

Note: This spelling analysis may not entirely apply to the written work of bilingual learners and learners who speak non-Standard varieties of English. The way the learner perceives the sounds and grammatical features of Standard English may show a need for more tuition in these areas and not indicate any perceptual processing weakness on the part of the learner. However, English spelling is not basically phonetic and learners need to understand the visual-motor nature of spelling.

Other points

- If a learner omits grammatical endings (e.g. -ed or -s), this is not necessarily because a learner doesn't 'hear' them; it may also be that the learner hasn't generalised the usage of these endings and may have difficulties with grammatical rules. In some cases it may be that they are motor errors, i.e. the learner has omitted these unintentionally. It is sometimes helpful not to code these sorts of errors until the end, when the learner's pattern of difficulties has emerged.

- Short vowel confusions, like *denner* for *dinner*, are not necessarily auditory errors. Often they may signify that the learner has difficulty remembering the 'rules' about appropriate letter combinations. Vowel sounds vary so much in English, depending on their context (e.g. 'a' in *cat, car, caught, bath*, etc.) that using them appropriately is often a matter of learning likely letter combinations and having a clear visual image of the word. This is especially true when the vowel is unstressed. Consequently, as a rule of thumb, coding such errors in Column C rather than Column D is less likely to be misleading.

- Learners may pronounce words differently according to where they live; for example learners from some parts of London may write 'birfday' for birthday. Such an error does not show a problem with sounds and is an acceptable phonetic rendering if their pronunciation is taken into account; it could therefore be categorised in Column C as it is primarily a problem of not following English spelling convention.

Planning a spelling programme

Identifying the patterns of difficulty a learner has is important in establishing an appropriate spelling programme.

Usually, through a spelling error analysis, a learner's strategies for attempting spelling will become clear, as will her strengths and weaknesses. For example, a learner who has most errors in Column C is tending to spell phonetically but is poor in remembering the visual elements of the word, and thus of acquiring a sense of when a word 'looks right'. In addition, such a learner shows a weakness in generalising from common spelling patterns and rules. This learner would need help in learning to use her phonic strengths, by inventing spelling pronunciations to help retrieve the visual image (e.g. par li a ment). She would also need help in understanding the structure of words and learning appropriate letter combinations, through word building and word 'families'.

On the other hand, a learner with most errors in Column D may be spelling visually but omitting or confusing sounds because she can't 'hear' or retain them. Such a learner would benefit from more visual approaches, such as emphasising letter patterns and finding words within words.*

---

* For a full discussion on setting up a spelling programme see Klein and Millar, 1990 and Klein, 1991.

References

Hulley, J. *Spelling Dictations*, Loxtrain, Sheffield College, 1992.

Klein, C. and Millar, R., *Unscrambling Spelling*, Hodder and Stoughton, 1990.

Klein, C. *Setting up a Learning Programme for Dyslexic Adults*, London Language and Literacy Unit, 1991.

Peters, M., *Diagnostic and Remedial Spelling Manual*, Macmillan Education, 1975.

Spelling to Learn: Using a learning styles approach to spelling with dyslexic adults (from adult dyslexia video series), London Language & Literacy Unit (see Resources).

Late one night my friend wrok me saying would you enjoy a tryk run in my new helpac I have had scealn sracbe in to my track suit before wore we were away the lights of the city glow ben to stars above I was beinging to wonder about are desigtion when I caught sight of the spinering knigh eagh of trul surface of what must have been a type of flying sauce wistering round use we dhic sillfulle to anoth a acciantence I suddele awoke in the comforley bed I had Λ acc luf.

An example of a dictation from a learner with auditory processing difficulties. Note the visual approach she takes as in *knigh* for *knife*. She generally has a good idea of acceptable letter combinations but can't always relate these appropriately to sound, as in *eagh* for *edge*. She has great difficulty tackling words when she has no visual image for them.

Lat one night my food friend walke me raying would you engoy a trial run in my new helicopter i had rearly rerambled into new trale rait befor we were way the ught of the city glowed benef the rtal abou doun . i war begunry to onedar about our lorrenatio wher i cout rit of the yenng knife edge of the s cirfir of what murt han been a type of flying coeer warding nound ur me the lodged rkilfully to around an ab acident to our relibe the rpace craft rugard hight and we rant doun to earth and the comefurtable bed i had never actualy left

An example of dictation from a learner with visual-motor processing difficulties. Note that the sounds are usually all there but visual elements are missing or confused and she is not very aware of the 'rules' of English spelling or what 'looks right'. She sometimes takes a lexical approach to spelling as in the creative spelling of *wonder* as *oneder*. Note also the handwriting difficulties, e.g. the 'spidery' quality, the incomplete or awkward construction of some letters and the lack of fluent joining (where the pen has stopped and then started again to look like joining letters). See Appendix V for correct version.

Spelling Error Analysis Chart

Date: ....

Learner's name: .... Dictation selection: ..... *Level 2* .....

Script	Error	A	B	C	D	E
late	lat			✓		
woke	walke					✓
enjoy	enjdy					✓
scarcely	skeasly				✓	
scrambled	skrambled			✓		
track	trak			✓		
before	befor	✓		✓		
lights	light				✓ or ✓	
beneath	benet			✓		
stars	star				✓ or ✓	
beginning	begining			✓		
wander	oneder			✓		
destination	dessination				✓	
caught	cort			✓		
sight	sit			✓		
spinning	spining			✓		
surface	cirfis			✓		
saucer	cocer			✓		
whistling	wiseling			✓		
skilfully	skillfully			✓		
avoid	avoud			✓ or ✓		
relief	relife		✓			
regained	regand			✓		
height	hight	✓		✓		
comfortable	comeferteble			✓		
actually	actualy					✓

A. Logical phonetic alternative and looks like an acceptable English spelling, i.e. follows English spelling convention (e.g. *spair/spare, tipe/type, prisition/precision*).

B. Visual-sequential (two letters within a word misordered, (e.g. *trail/trial, aviod/avoid*) where the confusion is visual rather than sound-based.

C. Shows lack of awareness of spelling rules or acceptable letter combinations (e.g. *babys* for *babies, apointed* for *appointed, pequler* for *peculiar, glod* for *glowed*).

D. Sounds are misheard or missing or missequenced (e.g. *sreet* for *street, divleved* for *delivered, cappalled* for *collapsed, theer* for *three*).

E. Motor: handwriting errors, such as omitting or repeating syllables or letters where the hand has not done what was intended, i.e. telescoping or perseverating (e.g. *rember* or *rememember* for *remember*), or unintentionally substituting one word for another.

Observations: Spidery handwriting, picks up pen or stops often between letters, so what looks like joining often isn't. Writes slowly. Seems to have poor visual memory for distinctive letter patterns and takes phonetic approach generally. Sometimes uses lexical knowledge as in 'oneder'. Unsure of many vowel combinations. Not keeping track of sentences as in omitting 'my' and omitting plurals – probably concentrating too much on spellings. Oblivious to punctuation.

Spelling Error Analysis Chart

Date: ....

Learner's name: .... Dictation selection: ....

Script	Error	A	B	C	D	E

A. Logical phonetic alternative and looks like an acceptable English spelling, i.e. follows English spelling convention (e.g. *spair/spare, tipe/type, prisition/precision*).

B. Visual-sequential (two letters within a word misordered, (e.g. *trail/trial, aviod/avoid*) where the confusion is visual rather than sound-based.

C. Shows lack of awareness of spelling rules or acceptable letter combinations (e.g. *babys* for *babies, apointed* for *appointed, pequler* for *peculiar, glod* for *glowed*).

D. Sounds are misheard or missing or missequenced (e.g. *sreet* for *street, divleved* for *delivered, cappalled* for *collapsed, theer* for *three*).

E. Motor: handwriting errors, such as omitting or repeating syllables or letters where the hand has not done what was intended, i.e. telescoping or perseverating (e.g. *rember* or *rememember* for *remember*), or unintentionally substituting one word for another.

Observations:

5 | Writing Analysis

A close analysis of one or more pieces of free writing is an important adjunct to a dictation. Such writing can reveal organisational and expressive language difficulties as well as handwriting difficulties which only occur in a longer written piece, such as letter construction breaking down or frequent 'dropping' of letters and words.

Ask the learner to bring a piece of writing, preferably from course work or employment, along to the diagnostic interview. It is useful if the learner has not used a dictionary for spellings and if it is a final draft, it helps to also see a first draft. Many learners have to rewrite course work several times to produce an acceptable draft. It can be of great value to see these and to explore the learner's experience of, and approach to, writing as part of the analysis.

It is particularly important to ensure a writing analysis is done on a piece of writing of appropriate length and difficulty to identify the full range of difficulty. If at all possible the piece of writing should be at least one side of A4, or longer depending on the learner's level.

If the learner is taking written exams, it is helpful to compare a piece of timed writing with one written in the learner's own time.

The following is a guide to identifying the kinds of difficulties which may contribute to a diagnosis of dyslexia.

However, it is important to view any writing difficulties in the context of the learner's experience of writing and in the light of reading, spelling and other difficulties.

Handwriting

Here you are looking for problems with motor coordination or integration as well as motor control.

- Does the learner do joined up writing? Is it regular in formation?
- How does she hold the pen? Does she press hard? Does she have difficulty controlling her writing?
- Does she have to concentrate on forming the letters? Is formation immature? Is writing slow and arduous?
- Does she confuse 'b' and 'd' or any other letters, or make any backwards, e.g. 2 for S?
- Does she mix up capital and lower case letters?
- Is the construction of letters awkward or confusing, e.g. open a's (α) or letters which are fused (ω for $\omega\iota$)?
- Does she frequently drop or add letters unintentionally?
- Is her handwriting irregular or variable in size and direction?

Spelling

It is helpful to analyse the spelling errors in a piece of writing alongside the spelling error analysis of the dictation, as there may be observations which add to the diagnostic picture. For example, inconsistency in spelling a word is more likely to show up in a piece of free writing, as are motor errors such as frequently omitting final letters unintentionally.

Punctuation

Dyslexic individuals have difficulty acquiring the conventions of language, such as punctuation.

- Does she use full stops appropriately? Commas?
- Does she seem to grasp when a sentence is complete? Can she make a sentence complete if it is not?
- Does she use apostrophes appropriately? Other punctuation?

Grammar and sentence structure

Dyslexic adults may have underlying language difficulties and/or sequencing problems which affect their acquisition of grammar and their sentence structure. This may be especially evident when they are trying to express complex ideas.

- Does she use tense consistently?
- Does she use subject–verb agreement consistently?
- Does she leave off grammatical endings, e.g. *-ed*?
- Is sentence structure awkward or confusing?
- Does she omit words that affect sentence structure?
- Does she use incorrect verb forms, e.g. *have being* for *have been*?
- Can she restructure sentences?

Vocabulary

- Does she use incorrect forms of words, e.g. *difficultness*?
- Does she confuse words with similar constructions, e.g. *underlying/underlining*?
- Does she frequently confuse meanings of words?

Written expression

Problems with word retrieval and/or underlying expressive language difficulties may affect the dyslexic writer's ability to express her intention in writing.

- Does she use roundabout expression to convey ideas?
- Does she use repetitive phrasing or words?
- Does she use simplified language to convey complex thoughts?
- Does she have problems finding the 'right' words or the 'right' way to say something?
- Is written expression generally confused or awkward, i.e. the ideas are 'there' but not clearly expressed?

Organisation and structure

Most dyslexic adults have difficulties planning and organising a piece of writing; these difficulties are more evident when organising complex ideas as in discursive writing.

- Does she have problems sequencing or putting ideas in order?
- Can she make and follow a plan?
- Does she use paragraphing appropriately?
- Can she:
    - keep to the point?
    - select main ideas?
    - expand an idea?
    - group ideas/categorise?
- Can she understand and apply conventions of formal written English, e.g. introduction and conclusion, use of transitional phrases?

Proof-reading and editing

- Does she write drafts/edit own work?
- Does she proof-read own work?
    - can she find errors?
    - can she correct errors?

An example of a piece of a psychology student's essay:

Schizophreina is the lable appied to a group of disorders, charcterized by servere personality disorganizhon, distortion of realty and an inability ro funchon in daily life.
Most experts belife. Schizophreina encompasses several disorders. Each of which may have a diffrent cause.
Schinozophrimia is the historcal term, and one still most commonly used.

63

It occures in all cultures, even those that are remote from the stress of Modern Civilization It appears to have played humanity throughout History.

Schizophreinia Usally appears in young adulthood, the peak ages are between 25-35. Experts are now looking back at these age groups. There is belifs that it may even start from birth "The schizophrenic child BY Dr Sheila Canton". Somhimes the disorders develop slowly as a gradual process of Increasing Seclusivness, and inapropriate behaviour. Somtimes it appears sudden, marked by intense Confusion. Wheather the disordr develops slowly or Suddenly, the symptor are many and varied. Schizophrenic individuals Usally fail to exsibit

A summary of a writing analysis of this writer would note the lack of joined up writing and the unevenness and large size and somewhat immature appearance of the writing. The spelling is erratic, e.g. *schizophrenia* is spelled several different ways throughout. Spelling errors indicate poor visual memory and some motor integration difficulties expressed through telescoping, as in *charcterized* and *disorganiztion*. The writing seems very abbreviated; she probably needs help with understanding the form and conventions of an essay, and she is not completely clear about paragraphing. She knows she's supposed to give references, but doesn't know how to do it. Her points are direct and appropriate but she needs to learn how to expand them, organise them into larger units and give examples. She is very unclear about the use of punctuation and grammar is hazy, as in, '*There is belifs*' and *sudden* rather than *suddenly*. She appears to need help with editing and proof-reading to 'see' her errors. Expressive language seems generally good but where she has written, 'Experts are now looking back at these age groups', she seems to actually mean that they are looking *beyond* these age groups at younger ones or that they are revising this view; she may therefore need help to develop more exact written expression.

6 | **Drawing Conclusions**

Anything which becomes clear at the interview should be shared with the individual at that time; often the learner's comments will help to illuminate her difficulties. The whole process, ideally, is tutor and learner looking together at the evidence accumulating in front of them. However, it is usually necessary to have time away to analyse and reflect at some length on the evidence to determine whether the learner is dyslexic and what sort of language processing problems are dominant.

At this stage, try to pull together all the information that has been collected and look at each aspect of the diagnosis in the light of all the others. Are there factors from the interview and the reading, writing and spelling analyses which suggest visual processing difficulties, visual confusions, a weak visual memory? Are there factors which suggest auditory processing problems, weak discrimination and blending skills, poor auditory memory? Are there factors which suggest poor motor integration, motor tracking? Are there patterns of difficulties with memorising, sequencing, direction, word retrieval? Are the difficulties specific, persistent and intractable in spite of the learner's efforts and perhaps extra help at school? Do other factors, such as second language interference or missing a lot of school, for example, seem to account for the difficulties, or do these seem inadequate to explain them? Are there significant discrepancies between the learner's oral and written abilities, and/or between her reading and spelling level?

Often, from a complete diagnostic assessment, the tutor can determine both whether the learner is dyslexic and whether the specific difficulties are primarily auditory or visual, and if there is a significant motor component. There is frequently a somewhat mixed picture, but the more specific you can be about where the learner's strengths and weaknesses lie, the more this will help to inform teaching strategies.

However, sometimes it is necessary to work with the learner over a period of time to observe the learner's *learning style*: is the learner a 'quick forgetter', does she have difficulties generalising, applying rules, remembering names or facts, as well as spellings, 'seeing' errors, coping with sequence and order? Do the difficulties persist in spite of appropriate tuition?

It is useful to remember that diagnosis is an art rather than a science; it is seeing how the various factors of a learner's difficulties form a learning *pattern* and what this reveals about a learner's strengths and weaknesses.

7 | Overview of Dyslexic Difficulties

The following are some general observations about characteristics that seem to go together. Not all are always true for adults who manifest these difficulties. They are indicators which can help to determine a pattern of difficulties.

Visual processing problems

Background

Look for incidence of squint or amblyopia as a child (ages 7–10). Possible unstable binocular control.

Reading

May have been able to learn to use phonic system just enough so not aware of difficulties until junior school. Others with severe directional and sequencing problems may have had problems earlier on.

Advanced readers: Jerky style. Visual tracking problems evident. Phonetic attack often fairly adequate. Sometimes they are aware they are 'poor' or 'slow' readers. Often misread familiar words.

Other levels: Have difficulties recognising words. Sometimes may read upside down with better comprehension.

Comprehension: May need to reread passage several times to remember significant details. Spontaneous recall is vague. There is usually a significant discrepancy between listening comprehension and reading comprehension.

General: Distracted by typographical errors, may not use punctuation cues, does not often correct errors or monitor comprehension. Lose their place easily. Sometimes print appears to 'jump' or 'blur', eyes may get very tired after reading only a short time.

Spelling

Majority of errors are phonetic alternatives, but often fail to follow English spelling convention. Weak memory for letters and spelling patterns.

Rule-based errors are common, e.g. *partys* for *parties*.

Visual sequencing errors may occur, e.g. *naer* for *near*.

Spelling frequently inconsistent, i.e. will spell a word several different ways in one piece of writing.

Handwriting

Handwriting may not be a problem although 'b'/'d' confusion may continue to exist in advanced writers; however, visual-motor difficulties often go together.

Other

Easily distracted visually. General directional confusions and visual sequencing problems common, e.g. confusing signs in maths (+/x) and place (decimals/long division). Difficulty seeing errors, proof-reading.

Auditory processing problems

Background

Look for evidence of ear infections, severe bouts of bronchitis or tonsillitis, glue ear (ages 3–8); minor speech difficulties; 'late talkers'.

Reading

Severe reading difficulties as children.

Advanced readers: Major problems in decoding unfamiliar words. Other than this can be quite fluent readers. Often have good comprehension if there are not too many unfamiliar words.

Other readers: Same as above, but many more errors; may need additional reading strategies.

General: Rely heavily on context, visual appearance and lexical 'chunks'. May use initial letter sounds to guess at words.

Have significant difficulty reading non-words.

Spelling

Often use visual approach. Phonetic approach generally unsuccessful.

Spellings frequently very disordered. Major sounds may be missing or confused, especially l/r blends; medial m/n, unaccented syllables.

Sequencing errors involving sound confusions are common, e.g. *gril* for *girl, fuirt* for *fruit.*

Syllables may be omitted or missequenced, e.g. *imediale* for *immediately, capalled* for *collapsed.*

Spellings are very difficult to acquire.

Handwriting

No significant problems.

Other

Phonological processing problems, e.g. difficulties segmenting and manipulating speech sounds, (as in a spoonerism task). May have difficulties with rhyme. Often distracted auditorially; also slow in processing aural information. Problems in maths often have to do with the language of maths.

Motor integration problems

Background

Look for coordination difficulties as children (especially eye/hand); articulation difficulties; handwriting problems.

Reading

May not have significant difficulties in reading, but may have problems crossing midline so need to put text to one side to read.

Visual tracking may be a problem.

Spelling

Many spellings phonetically accurate.

Spelling errors usually include:
– omission of syllables
– repetition of syllables or letters
– unintentional omission or addition of letters, or writing different letter than intended.

Handwriting

Handwriting not automatic and difficulties may be severe.

Constructional and directional problems may be evident.

May have to press hard to control writing.

May not be able to write fast enough to complete work, or express ideas adequately on paper; or letter construction may break down.

Other indications:
– lack of cursive writing
– scratchy or variable style
– inability to stay on the line
– irregular size, formation or fusing of letters.

Other

May not have attentional difficulties of those with auditory or visual problems.

Planning and organising difficulties, with essays, assignments, discursive writing, but also more generally, e.g. organising folders, time.

Often combined with visual processing problems (i.e. poor hand-eye coordination), sometimes auditory processing problems.

Persistent difficulties for most dyslexic adults

- Memorising names, facts
- Remembering sequences, e.g. alphabet, instructions
- Rote memory tasks in maths, e.g. times tables, basic number facts
- Right/left discrimination
- Learned to tell time late, may still have problems; also estimating time
- Concentration difficulties or easily distracted
- Severe expressive writing problems even when orally competent
- Difficulties with the conventions of written language
- Copying difficulties
- Word retrieval – getting ideas down on paper, also when speaking
- Pronunciation difficulties, especially with multisyllabic words.

8 | Writing Reports and Making Recommendations

The diagnostic report

It is important to write a diagnostic report for several reasons: it allows us as tutors to identity, clarify and summarise the learner's difficulties for ourselves and the learner, and to make recommendations for supporting the learner in the classroom and/or workplace, in examinations and in individual tuition.

When writing a report we need to consider why we are writing it (e.g. to get special examination provision, to recommend learning support, to obtain support for the learner from other tutors, to help the learner understand her difficulties) and who we are writing it for (e.g. the learner, tutors, employers, examining boards). The report should be written in accordance with all the relevant aims. A report for examination provision, for example, needs to clearly make the case for the kinds of difficulties the learner experiences in reading, writing and spelling, the persistent and specific nature of these difficulties in spite of appropriate tuition and how they are exacerbated under examination conditions.

In writing for other tutors, it is important to help them to see how learners' difficulties will affect them in the classroom, in their specific subject areas, and how they can be supported. When writing for workplace supervisors, the purpose is to help them understand how the difficulties affect the learner in their work and to suggest strategies and support which will enable the individual to succeed in the context of the workplace. It is important that tutors and supervisors, or others, understand the kind of difficulties dyslexic people have so they will not be misperceived as lazy, careless or incompetent.

It is also important to be sensitive to the learner's feelings about the report, to go through the report with her and be willing to change wording until the report is acceptable to her. Only those personal details that are necessary should be included and these should be put as generally as possible. For instance, one adult was upset by the comment that his mother also had these difficulties as he felt she was being 'blamed'. Changing the wording to 'other members of his family have similar difficulties' resolved the problem. Individuals need to 'own' their report; it is their report to use for their own purposes.

Recommendations

Examination boards, other examining bodies and higher education institutions make various provision in written examinations for learners with dyslexia. GNVQ, GCSE, 'A' level boards and others will generally grant extra time (25%) and rest breaks which can be arranged through the examination centre on the basis of a report written by a qualified teacher or educational psychologist. Centres should also provide separate accommodation. Time extensions beyond 25% and other provision such as an amanuensis, a reader or use of a word processor have to be agreed by the relevant examination board or other examining body and require appropriate evidence from a qualified practitioner. It is helpful to request that examiners give special consideration for spelling and written expression in examinations where this is allowable. The learner should be consulted about what provision she would like and it is important to talk through the options and to check regulations with examining bodies. If using an amanuensis, it is important that the learner practises with the amanuensis ahead of time so is able to use the support well. It is helpful for learners to practise using any provision offered, for example extra time, so they use it effectively.

Recommendations should be directly linked to specific difficulties and would include some or most of the following, in addition to any examination provision.

(i) Follow a course of study making regular reading and writing demands (if not already doing this) in order to get the practice needed to develop these skills. The learner should be encouraged to use the words she wants in her writing rather than stay confined by the words she can spell.

(ii) Receive regular one-to-one specialist learning support to work on their specific language and learning needs. Dyslexic learners often have great difficulty applying conventions and procedures and need support in practising them in their own writing. They usually need help with note taking, planning and organising writing, editing and proof-reading. An individually-structured spelling programme* may also be recommended. Most dyslexic learners need to learn spellings and gain confidence from developing effective strategies for remembering spellings.

A spelling programme often provides a core of the support work which reveals more clearly to learner and teacher, the learner's particular learning style and needs, and can demonstrate constantly why a learner needs to learn in a particular way. The spelling programme gives immediate rewards if done properly; the multisensory learning and systematic revision works for most learners, particularly if the strategies for remembering are tailored to their perceptual strengths.

The learner may also need support on devising strategies for improving reading. The spelling programme can often help with reading; the visual chunking gives an alternative approach to someone who can't sound out, and it can also help build word recognition. However, the learner may also need to develop comprehension techniques for reading. In addition, for a learner suffering visual stress, a sheet of coloured acetate (in a preferred colour) placed over a page can reduce glare or 'blurring' or 'jumping', and a card under or above the line being read can aid visual tracking.

Specific maths or numeracy support may be needed; this should be appropriate to the learner's course, employment or other aims.

The learner may also need help with organising folders, work and/or time.

---

*Such a programme is outlined in Klein and Millar, *Unscrambling Spelling* and Klein, *Setting up a learning programme for dyslexic adults.*

(iii) Receive classroom support from subject tutors; for instance, giving the learner copies of their notes, extra time for assignments, ensuring handouts are easy to read and/or printed on the learner's preferred colour, developing proof-reading skills through error analysis marking of learner's written work. Subject tutors should also be sensitive to the dyslexic learner's spelling and expressive writing difficulties and mark for content wherever possible.

(iv) Technological support such as the use of voice recognition technology or other software, a 'reading pen', the loan of a laptop or cassette recorder may also be appropriate. Learners may also need training and support in using any technology.

(v) Other support such as extra time on loans of library or learning centre resources.

(vi) A learner may have other immediate needs revealed by the interview for which a recommendation may be helpful. For instance, provision of a quiet place was recommended for a work-based trainee who had to work where loud music was played and who had severe auditory processing difficulties.

The learning support tutor may need to liaise or help the learner liaise with other staff; consequently, great care should be given to making recommendations, as they offer a basis and structure for supporting the learner and an opportunity to ensure a programme and network of support that can enable the learner to succeed and reach her potential.

The following is an example of a diagnostic report by a specialist dyslexia support tutor in adult community education provision. The learner is following courses in literacy and computing, and in bookkeeping.

R was referred by her literacy tutor because of persistent difficulties with spelling and reading.

Background

R remembers having problems learning to read and write at primary school and these problems continued into secondary school. Despite this she received no extra help during her school career. She left at 15 without taking any exams. R has a son with similar difficulties, who has been diagnosed with dyslexia.

In her interview, R reported many of the difficulties commonly associated with dyslexia. She reports memorisational difficulties and has difficulty remembering telephone numbers, instructions and things she needs to do. She constantly makes lists to remind her of everyday tasks that need completing. She sometimes chants information in order to remember it, although not always with success. She has difficulty recalling names and dates. Although she can recite the alphabet, she is unable to say what comes after a particular letter without going back to the beginning. She was unable to say the months of the year backwards. She is generally very good at maths, but has never been able to learn her multiplication tables. R also exhibits some left/right confusion and directional problems. She reported that she often mixes up the letters 'b' and 'd', and sometimes reverses 'u' and 'n', and she has to pick up a pen to know which is her right hand.

R finds it hard to concentrate when there is any background noise. She generally has trouble taking in rapid auditory information, and finds using the phone particularly difficult. This causes her problems at work where she is expected to take down credit card authorisation numbers over the telephone. She finds it hard to listen and write down notes at the same time. R also has some pronunciation difficulties; she correctly repeated three out of the four multisyllabic words I gave her, but reported that she is aware of having pronunciation difficulties (for example she says *emotion* as *emulsion*). This was also evident during the course of the interview when she said *contents* for *context*, *exsorb* for *absorb* and *pecific* for *specific*. She often has difficulty finding the words she wants when she speaks. These are all indicators of auditory processing difficulties.

Reading

R tries to read novels for pleasure but reports being a slow reader. She says she often 'loses the story' and has to reread in order to understand. She finds it difficult to work out unknown words and she tends to 'put her own words in' to fit the context. For this assessment R read a GCSE level text, making 36 miscues. She read in a fairly fluent style and despite the high number of miscues her comprehension was good. She understood the main points and remembered some of the detail. She corrected five of her miscues, usually by repeating phrases. She generally observed punctuation although in one case she read a comma as a full stop which interfered with her understanding of that sentence. Two thirds of her miscues showed high semantic strength and 70% showed high syntactic strength.

The fact that R reads fairly fluently suggests she is taking a visual approach to word recognition but this approach is not always successful and she substitutes visually similar words, for example *glimmer* for *glitter* and *proceeded* for *persisted* which keep the sense of the passage, indicating her reliance on context.

R's longest hesitations occur when she approaches an unknown word. She attempts a phonetic attack but this is usually unsuccessful. For example, on two occasions she omitted a word after an attempt at the first syllable.

R scored 7 out of 20 in the Long Regular Word List. She tried to phonetically decode the words she did not recognise but was unable to attempt some words and with other words she managed only the first sound or syllable. Where she did attempt to read the whole word, the sounds were often confused.

R scored 4 out of 10 for the one-syllable items in the Snowling Graded Non-word Reading Test. She has problems blending the initial consonants; for example she read *drant* as *durand* and *trolb* as *terold* (notice the misreading of the final 'b' as 'd', showing directional confusions). She managed only 2 out of 10 two-syllable items. The scores for these tests confirm she has difficulties with phonological processing.

R only recognised 6 out of 22 words previously known to her in the Irregular Word List. Her low score indicates some difficulties with visual word recognition. When reading words on the Irregular Word List that she did not recognise, R produced visually similar words; for example, she read *naïve* as *native*, and *thyme* as *theme*. She also looked for words within words; for example she read *placebo* as *place-do* (notice how she has again misread the 'b' as a 'd'), *banal* as *ban-all* and *simile* she remarked was '*smile with an extra i*'.

Her reading indicates considerable auditory processing difficulties with some added weaknesses in visual memory.

Spelling

R was given Margaret Peters' intermediate level dictation in which she made errors in 26 out of 100 words. More than half of these showed evidence of auditory processing problems, with sounds missequenced, misheard or missing. For example, she spelled *scrambled* as *sramabled*, *caught* as *cal* and *destination* as *desation*. Of her errors, 23% showed a lack of awareness of spelling rules or acceptable letter patterns. For example, she wrote *regand* for *regained* and *dodged* for *doged*. Her spelling of *trial* as *trail*, *edge* as *egde* and *avoid* as *aviod* showed a poor memory for visual sequences.

This pattern of errors would suggest that R's main problems when trying to spell are auditory processing difficulties, but these are compounded by some visual processing difficulties. Consistent with this, R was able to identify, but not correct, 65% of her errors while she mis-identified *beneath* as an error.

Writing

R produced a piece of free writing of about 300 words for the assessment. She writes in a legible, semi-cursive script with some letters poorly constructed. The piece had several spelling errors. There is a significant discrepancy between R's oral and written expression. She used short, simple sentences, which makes her writing rather stilted. Although she expressed herself fairly clearly, there were examples of awkward expression and confused tenses and the piece lacked descriptive words and phrases. There is some repetition of vocabulary and it is sometimes similar to verbal expression in style. R reports that her difficulties with spelling limit her written expression. R starts a piece of writing without prior organisation, planning and drafting. She seems unclear about paragraphing, although it is attempted.

Other assessments

R's score in the digit span test (9 out of 17) was below average. She had particular difficulties with repeating numbers backwards, and was only able to do four digits. R was asked to do a phonological processing task which involves manipulating sounds in common names by changing the initial sounds in each word to create a spoonerism, for example Jack Dee to Dack Jee. R found this extremely difficult and took over two minutes to attempt four names; she was able to do only one correctly, after which we abandoned the task. She seemed to approach the task by visualising how the new word would look and then she would try pronouncing it. For example with the name she got right, *Mike Tyson*, she said 'that's *T* and then *ike*, I don't know how you say that, oh *Tike*'. Her difficulties are a clear indication of auditory processing problems.

Conclusions and recommendations

There is clear evidence that R has dyslexia. Her primary weakness is her auditory processing difficulty compounded by visual processing difficulties. Having said that, R is articulate and hardworking and despite her difficulties she has compensated well in reading. Her reading difficulties will be more evident in cases where she needs to read out of context. Her writing and spelling, however, remain extremely weak and because of this her written work is not representative of her knowledge or understanding.

I recommend R is given one-to-one specialist dyslexia support, to work on her reading and writing needs. This support should be as follows.

- To improve her spelling and increase her word recognition when reading, R should have a structured spelling programme based on the Look, Cover, Say, Write and Check method. This should employ her lexical and relative visual and motor strengths rather than relying on auditory strategies. R should be encouraged to use the spell check facility on the word processor.
- R should be given support in the reading and comprehension of texts in the final part of her bookkeeping course.
- The structure and language of narrative texts should be made explicit to R, and this, along with the development of her sight vocabulary, should improve R's comprehension and enjoyment of novels and other narratives.
- In writing, R should be given instruction in the use of formal conventions.
- R needs support in organising her writing. She should have support with learning how to plan, draft and edit her work. She should make full use of the cut and paste facility on the word processor to assist her with this.
- R should be helped to develop proof-reading strategies and should proof-read her work separately for her 'danger points', such as leaving off '-ed' endings.
- R needs to develop her expressive written language. Building up kernel sentences and using the computer thesaurus will be beneficial here.
- Punctuation and grammar problems should be dealt with in the context of developing her writing.

The work she does in specialist support should be reinforced in her literacy class, where she should be encouraged to write as much as possible.

In addition:
As R finds it difficult to listen and take notes from the board, she should be given printed handouts in all of her classes or she should be allowed to tape-record the lesson.

If R goes on to take written examinations she should be given 25% extra time. This will give her the extra time she needs when reading to enable a full understanding of the questions and to plan and proof-read her writing.

She should be given sympathetic consideration of her spelling difficulties in examinations and assessed course work. If possible she should be permitted to use a word processor in exams to help with spelling, planning, editing and proof-reading her writing.

I would be glad to advise on any additional ways R's tutors can support her.

Dyslexia Support Tutor

References

Klein, C. and Millar R., *Unscrambling Spelling,* Hodder and Stoughton, 1990.

Klein C., *Setting up a learning programme for dyslexic adults,* London, Language and Literacy Unit, 1991.

9 | Telling a Learner About Dyslexia

After having a diagnostic session, many learners want to know more about the how and why of their condition. Dyslexia is a disability or specific difficulty which needs to be identified and clarified with the learner. This is not because of some desire to label learners, but because adults need to understand that their difficulties will not go away with tuition, practice or hard work. If the learner is an adult with severe spelling difficulties, she will always have spelling difficulties. Adults deserve to be told what we understand to be their difficulties, the hardships these may impose on them, and the support they are entitled to. They also need to be assured that they have strengths as well as weaknesses, and can learn, improve and succeed in spite of these difficulties.

Some adults are shocked to discover the extent of their difficulties and need many hours of support and guidance to come to terms with what dyslexia means to them. On the other hand, a substantial number of adults are relieved to have their difficulties acknowledged and explained, to find that others have the same kinds of difficulties they have and that educators are concerned about improving teaching and support for dyslexic learners.

Some adults are not interested in exploring their disability further and the diagnosis and teaching or examination recommendations may be enough for these learners.

The tutor should discuss the diagnosis in detail before moving on to a discussion of dyslexia.

Explaining the diagnosis

In discussing the diagnosis, many points will have come up during the diagnostic interview. Adults will often begin to make connections between their different difficulties during the interview and this should be encouraged. For instance, one learner began to see how her difficulties in copying were related to her other difficulties; another, how mistakes in telling the time were part of the dyslexic pattern.

It is useful in discussing the diagnosis to help the learner understand her strengths and weaknesses as a way of laying the basis for setting up a learning programme. In talking through the reading analysis it is helpful to show the learner, for example, that her difficulty with comprehension is because she must try so hard to work out the look and sound of a word that she does not pay enough attention to meaning and grammatical structure. This can be done by using Venn diagrams (see Helen Arnold, 1982) or some other method to show the learner the kinds of miscues she made and explain what these mean. You might want to show another learner how she is using meaning and syntax to predict because she can't seem to decode the words; this may be a good way into talking about her difficulty in discriminating sounds or translating letters into sounds.

A similar approach can be taken with spelling. Learners often find it very revealing and reassuring to categorise their own errors;* they then realise that they make certain types of mistakes and that there is a 'method' in their approach to spelling.

Dyslexic learners also benefit from understanding that their organisational, planning and sequencing difficulties are part of the pattern of difficulties and not just a result of laziness or carelessness on their part. To discover that getting lost, being late or disorganised may also be connected to their reading and spelling difficulties can also help release them from a sense of guilt and failure and enable a new confidence.

It is also important to go through a written report with individuals because seeing their difficulties spelled out in print can be distressing even though these have been previously acknowledged.

---

* A discussion on this, along with a form for learners to use, can be found in Klein & Millar, 1990.

Explaining dyslexia

For learners who want to know more about dyslexia there are a number of approaches which can offer a jumping off point from which to explore the subtle nature of dyslexia. These approaches are by no means the only ways to discuss dyslexia (dyslexic adults among themselves are often better at it), but offer possible guidelines for a tutor to begin.

For all these explanations, it is important that the tutor stresses that dyslexia has nothing to do with intelligence. Before embarking on the following explanations, it is advisable to do some additional reading on the brain. (See Carter, 1998; Greenfield, 1997 and Springer and Deutch, 1998.)

1. The Brain *(see diagram overleaf)*

When talking about the brain and language processing, it is helpful to link them to individual difficulties which the learner has spoken about in the interview. It is also useful to emphasise the different role of the left and right hemispheres in processing written language. (See *Demystifying Dyslexia* for some useful materials in exploring these further.)

This drawing of the brain has purposefully been made very simple so that you can draw on it as appropriate. One way of using it is the following:

(a) If the learner appears to have auditory perceptual problems, indicate how auditory information is processed.

1. Information goes into the ears (learner can hear).

2. Indicate which area of the brain processes certain auditory information, e.g. left – language, right – music, environmental sounds, etc. (Note: this is a useful distinction though it is a simplification.)

3. Show how some messages are sent directly to the language centre on the same side (ipsi-lateral) but most are sent over the corpus callosum to the other side (contra-lateral) and this is the main route.

4. Explain that there is a problem in the processing or retrieval of auditory information having to do with language. It may be helpful to show that there are different parts of the brain which process different aspects of language in the left hemisphere and that it is specific aspects of language which are difficult, e.g. breaking a word into speech sounds (refer here to difficulties with spoonerisms).

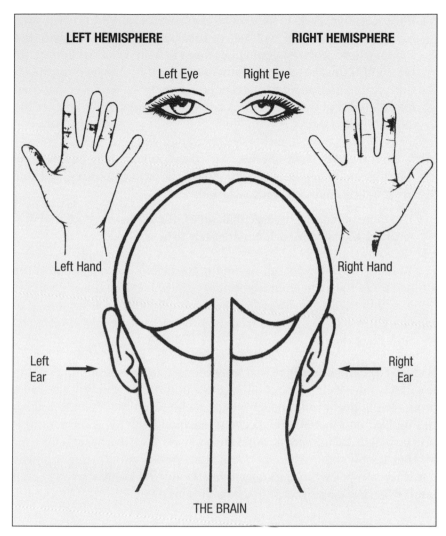

LEFT HEMISPHERE   RIGHT HEMISPHERE

Left Eye   Right Eye

Left Hand   Right Hand

Left Ear →   ← Right Ear

THE BRAIN

(b) If the learner appears to have visual processing difficulties, use the same process as (a) except via the eyes. (Note that visual processing involves the left and right visual fields of both eyes.) Explain that the right hemisphere mainly processes images but the left hemisphere is where letters and words are linked to their sounds. That is why the learner may be good at remembering images and patterns but poor at remembering spellings. Explain that the learner may have problems retrieving a visual sequence of letters, or recognising words in print.

(c) If the learner appears to have motor control problems the problem area is in the motor strip on each side of the corpus callosum. Explain that she may have problems getting her hand to write what she intends, or her mouth to say the word she wants to say. It may help to explain that visual and auditory perception is the way we take in verbal information, but we need to speak or write to express it; this is where the difficulties lie.

(d) If several areas seem affected, e.g. visual-motor, then explain how information is processed from one area of the brain to another, and how eye-hand coordination can be affected.

The more severe the dyslexic difficulties, the more areas are probably involved. Usually several areas are likely to be affected.

e) You may wish to point out where the cerebellum is (behind and at the bottom of the main brain (cerebrum) and explain that this plays a part in making skills *automatic*. Here you can refer to the learner's need to concentrate on forming letters, for example, so she 'loses' what she wants to write.

It should be emphasised here that learners need to understand that we are not discussing their intellectual abilities but rather specific aspects in processing linguistic information. It can be helpful to say that the learner has misfiled information and specialist teaching helps file it correctly. It is also helpful to discuss specific problems such as how a learner can miscopy and not identify errors when she doesn't have a good visual memory, or why a learner can spell when she knows what the words look like but can't even guess when she doesn't because she can't 'sound out'.

It is especially useful here to talk about dyslexia as a 'difference' in the way the brain is organised, and that it is a problem when doing tasks connected with some aspects of language. In most people the left hemisphere has developed to specialise in speech and language functions. This left side of the brain works in an analytical, sequential way. The right side of the brain specialises in visual-spatial thinking and functions in a holistic way. Some studies indicate that the dyslexic brain may be more symmetrical and less specialised for language. Current research suggests that many dyslexic people are more 'right brained', visual-spatial and holistic thinkers and this puts them at a disadvantage in a culture where written language is given the highest priority and status. It is useful here to relate this to the learner's own particular strengths and weaknesses. It can be helpful to use the analogy of the face – what comes first? The eyes? The mouth? The chin? The difficulties of putting a face into a sequence are similar to those the dyslexic person experiences in trying to organise language.

2. Written language processing

Some languages (Chinese for example) are analogic, that is they use pictographs that visually indicate what the word means (e.g. 人 looks a bit like a man). In English the word *man* does not look like a man at all but is rather a collection of three symbols to represent the 'sounds' we make when we say *man*. These symbols, m-a-n, are arbitrary and have no particular 'meaning' in relation to the word *man*; they are therefore more difficult to learn and must be learned by memorising. Memorising arbitrary symbols as in m-a-n, or other information such as facts or dates with no meaningful associations, rely on the 'working memory' to store and retrieve (or 'file') them. This contrasts with long-term memory which is based on meaning and association of ideas or images. Dyslexic people have difficulties with memorising but often have a good long-term memory; they can learn well when an activity has meaning and they can make meaningful connections. This is why they need different strategies to learn.

A further explanation of the working memory system, i.e. the 'visual-spatial sketchpad' and the 'phonological loop' (see McLoughlin et al, 2002) may also help dyslexic adults understand why they may have a good memory for faces and landmarks but not be able to remember names or follow directions. It may also help them understand why they have 'good days' and 'bad days', i.e. because of memory 'overload'.

These are two of the most meaningful ways of explaining the neurological and cognitive aspects of dyslexia to use with adults. These approaches need far more development with learners; I have given only guidelines here. Adults may wish to know more about dyslexia. Discussions about what dyslexia is may become an ongoing part of learning support, helping learners to make sense of their difficulties and why and how specialist tuition and particular strategies can help. It is very important to communicate to learners that their difficulties have meaning and can be understood, that they have other strengths and that they can learn.

References

Arnold, H., *Listening to Children Read*, Hodder & Stoughton, 1982.

Carter, R., *Mapping the Mind*, Weidenfeld and Nicolson, 1998.

Greenfield, S., *The Human Brain*, Weidenfeld and Nicolson, 1997.

Klein, C. and Millar, R., *Unscrambling Spelling*, Hodder & Stoughton, 1990.

Krupska, M. and Klein, C., *Demystifying Dyslexia*, London Language & Literacy Unit (available from Avanti), 1995.

McLoughlin, D., Leather, C. and Stringer, P., *The Adult Dyslexic: Interventions and outcomes*, Whurr, 2002.

Springer, S. and Deutch, G., 5th edition, *Left Brain, Right Brain*, W.H. Freeman and Co., 1998.

Appendix I
The Reading Process

'Reading is a matter of extracting, relating and processing cues to decode a precise message.' (Marie Clay)

In order to diagnose a learner's difficulties in reading and to identify strengths and weaknesses in reading it is necessary to be clear about how efficient readers read, how reading strategies develop in learners and how language processing difficulties may affect readers.

Defining and describing the reading process has not been an easy task and a number of conflicting theories have arisen in the attempt, all emphasising different aspects of the process and based on a variety of models and research in different areas.

Frank Smith, Kenneth Goodman and others from a background of psycholinguistics have described the reading process as a 'psycholinguistic guessing game' which 'involves an interaction between thought and language' (Goodman, 1967). They claimed that the fluent reader uses a minimum of clues from written material to arrive at meaning, 'sampling' a piece of writing on the basis of the knowledge they bring to it, and confirming and predicting from their knowledge of linguistic structures and meaning. Goodman wrote, 'Efficient reading does not result from precise perception and identification of all elements, but from a skill in selecting the fewest most productive cues necessary to produce guesses which are right first time. The ability to anticipate that which has not been seen, of course, is vital in reading, just as the ability to anticipate what has not yet been heard is vital in listening.' It followed from this model that the beginning reader or the poor reader would rely more heavily on graphic cues and that the fluent and experienced reader would rely more on prediction from context and less on graphic cues.

Although few people would disagree that reading is an interactive process, research suggests that fluent processing of written language relies on rapid word recognition rather than context, and that it is the poor reader who needs to rely more heavily on context. 'Recent evidence and argument goes against the long-held opinion that context aids word recognition and suggests instead that skilled readers are content to use rapid, efficient stimulus-driven processes to extract meaning from print' (Ellis, 1984). More recently, Marilyn Jager Adams (Adams, 1990) wrote, 'Laboratory research indicates that the most critical factor beneath fluent word reading is the ability to recognise letters, spelling patterns and whole words effortlessly, automatically and visually. The central goal of all reading instruction – comprehension – depends critically on this ability.'

Research in cognitive psychology suggests that efficient readers have an internal lexicon which they access by rapid and automatic sight recognition. They use context to construct meaning from words as they read, to compensate for slow or incomplete lexical access to difficult words, to select from alternative word meanings and to detect errors. However, this is very different from using context to predict, which is actually a rather slow and unnecessarily laborious method of reading, and not always successful. This can be shown by the passage below, where Polish words have been inserted throughout the text to simulate words the reader does not recognise and cannot 'decode', so that the reader must rely on context for working out words.

> Czytanie, jak thinking, is a zkomplikowany process. Whcn ty myślisz, all you have to do jest to produkować the responses from within you. Kiedy you read you have to produce responses które są precisely the ones the author pisał. You have to match twoje mysli do autora.

It is worth remembering that even if we can read by using context and minimal visual cues, that is not necessarily the way we *do* read. The disadvantage of reading like this should be apparent to anyone who has tried to read a photocopied piece of writing where some words were smudged or faint, or some letters missing at the end or beginning of each line.

The developmental perspective

The learner reader, however, does need to use context on the way to becoming a proficient reader. It is also important to note that children learning to read will pass through stages where they use different strategies. The emerging or pre-reading stage, according to Linnea Ehri, is when children learn about print and reading and 'learn the shapes and sounds of most alphabet letters...and acquire rudimentary awareness of sounds in words.'

The first stage of reading is the *initial reading* or decoding stage when they learn 'how the spelling system represents spoken language', i.e. the letter-sound system. The two predictors of success at this stage are letter-name knowledge and phonemic segmentation skill. Even at this stage, the better readers look at letters to guess words rather than guess using context.

In the second stage, the *fluency* stage, children become faster at decoding unfamiliar words, read known words more easily and faster, and integrate word reading with text comprehension processes. They develop the ability to 'read sight words as rapidly as they can name single letters or digits, indicating that sight words are being processed as single units rather than letter by letter.'

In the third stage, the *reading to learn* stage, they can read well enough 'to comprehend more difficult material whose ideas are unfamiliar.' Also at this stage, 'intelligence is more highly correlated with reading skill...and the amount of reading that students do becomes a major determiner of differences that distinguish good from poor readers.'

Research shows that 'students who have difficulty learning to read are almost always deficient in their knowledge about the spelling system and in their ability to read sight words effectively' (Ehri, 1991).

The two routes to reading

Uta Frith's model of the acquisition of literacy suggests three stages, which may overlap: the *logographic* stage, where words are identified by distinguishing visual features; the *alphabetic* stage, based on phoneme awareness where the letter-sound system is mastered; the *orthographic* stage which is based on visual analysis and is independent of sound (Snowling, 1985).

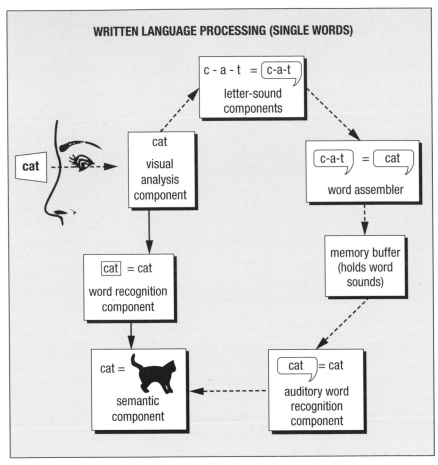

Adapted from 'How the brain copes with words', *New Scientist*, September 1985.

Researchers and theorists (see Jackson and Coltheart, 2001) have identified two routes of reading, which have been shown to operate independently, although each route aids in the development of the other: these are the *phonological* and the *visual* routes. The phonological or 'mediated' route corresponds to Frith's alphabetic stage: the reader, 'sounds out' the word. The visual or 'immediate' route corresponds to her orthographic stage. The diagram on the previous page shows a simplified model of the reading of single words. It is easy to see that the visual route (from word recognition to meaning) is more direct.

Using Frith's model it is possible to hypothesise that a reader may 'get stuck' at the alphabetic stage because of visual processing difficulties and never become skilled in word recognition. Such a reader may need to rely on 'sounding out', a slower and less satisfactory route which also impedes comprehension because the reader's attention is concentrated on the complex process of working out the words rather than constructing and monitoring meaning.

The following is an attempt to show what it is like to read by sounding out rather than recognising words:

Wreeding in thiss weigh menes yoo mussed konsentrait on sownding out eech werd sow itt wood bee difecult too komprehende a longue passudge.

It is also possible to identify the reader who fails to master the alphabetic stage because of phonological processing difficulties, and in spite of 'leapfrogging' to the orthographic stage, is never able to use the phonological route when faced with unfamiliar words or as a monitoring device. Because the letter-sound system is never mastered, knowledge about the spelling system is weak and cannot be used effectively to aid word recognition.

Some researchers refer to these two types of readers as the 'Phoenician' and the 'Chinese' readers. The 'Phoenician' reader relies 'more heavily than the average reader on phonic mediation,' whereas the 'Chinese' reader 'relies heavily on whole-word visual identification.' However, 'extreme Chinese and Phoenician readers are rare animals. The normal pattern is for a person to be good, mediocre or poor at both whole-word and phonic processing.' When looking at dyslexic reading styles, however, 'we are looking at relative not absolute development of differential whole word and phonic recognition skills.' (Ellis, 1984.)

The interactive-compensatory model

Frank Smith and Kenneth Goodman may be seen as proposing a 'top-down' or language-based view of reading, suggesting that readers look for meaning first, 'rather than strive to identify letters or words' (Smith, 1978). Thus readers would start at the 'top' or higher level of meaning and work 'down' to the lower levels of words and letters. They proposed this view in response to the 'bottom-up' view that decoding is central to reading development. This view proposes that readers analyse what they read initially at the level of visual features, then letter patterns corresponding to sound units and finally word perception, working up to meaning last. Although the 'bottom-up' view does not take into account readers' knowledge about language, research has shown that the 'top-down' or language-based view does not give an accurate picture of the skilled reader's use of rapid word recognition, and that it is inefficient to read by prediction.

More recently, (see Snowling, 1987) others have proposed an interactive-compensatory model, whereby both 'bottom-up' and 'top-down' processes are going on simultaneously. According to the interactive view, information from the printed page is processed 'bottom-up' starting from letters, then words, clause meanings and so on. However, the reader also has expectations which act 'top-down' toward lower levels. 'The essence of the interactive view is that high-level processes constrain low-level ones. Stanovitch has pointed out an interesting implication of the interactive view; namely, that normal processes at one level can compensate for deficient processes at another level. For example, if somebody were poor at the low-level skill of word identification, they would rely more heavily on high-level factors such as sentence context' (Jorm, 1983).

Stanovitch argues that children do 'use context in a compensatory manner so that when decoding skill is poor, and therefore proceeds slowly, context facilitates processing. When decoding becomes automatic and therefore proceeds rapidly, context has no effect' (Snowling, 1987).

Jorm (1983) comments that the finding that poor readers 'make greater use of context to aid word identification is surprising because...they are generally poorer at comprehension as well as word identification...They are often poorer at predicting a missing word on the basis of the preceding context...However, there is a crucial difference between being able to predict from context and actually making use of this capability. Although normal readers can make better predictions from context, they make less use of this skill in word identification. The reason that normal readers rely less on context is that they do not have the same need for it because they can identify words quite well on the basis of their visual features.' The fluent reader uses context primarily for error detection and monitoring meaning. 'The fluent reader needs to know if the text being read makes sense and matches expectation; and if it does not meet these criteria, whether the fault lies with the author, the mechanism of transmission (e.g. a misprint) or the reader...' (P. Smith, 1986).

'The compensatory hypothesis is important not only because it gives a description of the reading strategies used by (poor) readers, but also because ...it may be possible to help (them) to rely more heavily on those components of the reading process in which they are not deficient' (Jorm, 1983).

This means that the learner with weak word recognition or decoding skills may need to be encouraged to make better use of context to predict and monitor their reading. The interactive-compensatory model is thus a useful one, not only for understanding the reading process, but also for suggesting strategies to help poor readers compensate for their weaknesses.

References

Adams, M.J., *Beginning to Read*, MIT Press, 1990.

Ehri, L., 'The development of reading and spelling in children: an overview', in Snowling, M. and Thomson, M. (ed.) *Dyslexia: Integrating Theory and Practice*, Whurr, 1991.

Ehri, L.C., McCormack, S., 'Phases of word learning: Implications for instruction with delayed and disabled readers', *Reading and Writing Quarterly*, 14, 135-163, 1998.

Ellis, A., *Reading, Writing and Dyslexia*, Lawrence Erlbaum Associates, 1984, and 1993, 2nd edition.

Goodman, K., 'Reading: A psycholinguistic guessing game', *Journal of the Reading Specialist*, May 1967.

Jackson, N.E. and Coltheart, M., *Routes to Reading Success and Failure*, USA: Psychology Press, 2001.

Jorm, A.F., *The Psychology of Reading and Spelling Difficulties*, Routledge and Kegan Paul, 1983.

Smith, F., *Understanding Reading*, Holt, Rinehart and Winston, 1978.

Smith, P.T. 'The development of reading: the acquisition of a cognitive skill' in Fletcher, P. and Garman, M. (ed), *Language Acquisition*, Cambridge University Press, 1986.

Snowling, M., 'The assessment of reading and spelling skills', in Snowling, M., *Children's Written Language Difficulties*, NFER-Nelson, 1985.

Snowling, M., *Dyslexia: A Cognitive Developmental Perspective*, Basil Blackwell, 1987.

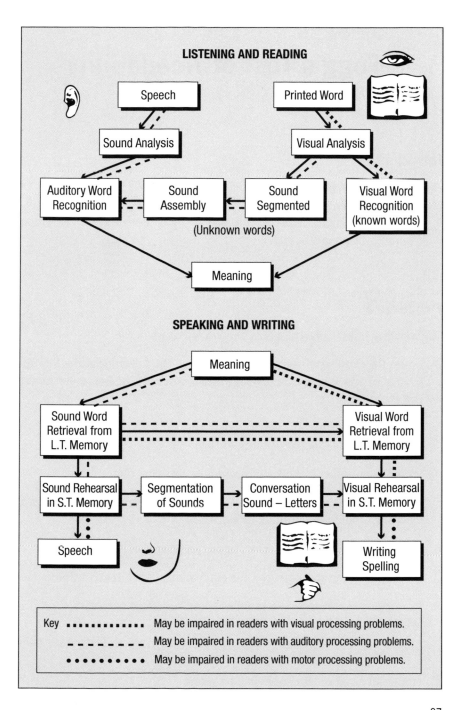

LISTENING AND READING

Speech → Sound Analysis

Printed Word → Visual Analysis

Sound Analysis → Auditory Word Recognition

Visual Analysis → Sound Segmented, Visual Word Recognition (known words)

Sound Segmented → Sound Assembly → Auditory Word Recognition

(Unknown words)

Auditory Word Recognition → Meaning ← Visual Word Recognition (known words)

SPEAKING AND WRITING

Meaning

Sound Word Retrieval from L.T. Memory

Visual Word Retrieval from L.T. Memory

Sound Rehearsal in S.T. Memory — Segmentation of Sounds — Conversation Sound – Letters — Visual Rehearsal in S.T. Memory

Speech

Writing Spelling

Key

•••••••••••• May be impaired in readers with visual processing problems.

– – – – – – – May be impaired in readers with auditory processing problems.

• • • • • • • • • • May be impaired in readers with motor processing problems.

97

Fogg's Test of Readability

Introduction

A quick and convenient method of checking levels of reading difficulty of any material with 100+ words giving reading age equivalents. It tends, however, to give high results so this should be taken into account when determining the level of a text.

Procedure

1. Take any sample of 100 words in complete sentences.

2. Count the number of sentences by counting the full stops; if the last full sentence stops short of the 100th word, count only the full sentences for this stage.

3. Count the number of words with three or more syllables. Omit capitalised words such as names; answer = y.

4. Divide the number of sentences into 100; answer = x.

5. Add the number of words with more than three syllables to your answer, i.e. x + y; y being the number of words.

6. Multiply x + y by 0.3 to give an American grade equivalent.

7. Add 5.0 to your answer to give the equivalent to an English reading age.

8. Example = four complete sentences and nine words with three or more syllables.
   a) $100 \div 4 = 25$ b) $25 + 9 = 34$ c) $34 \times 0.3 = 10.2$ d) $10.2 + 5 = 15.2$

The material has a reading age of c. 15 years.

Reading Age Level of Materials Based on Fogg Index
Sample size = 100 words

Number of Sentences (N)

Number of 3 Syll-a-ble words (S)	4	6	8	10	12	14	16	18	20	22	24	26	28	30	32	34
0	12.5	10.0	8.8	8.0	7.5	7.1	6.9	6.7	6.5	6.4	6.3	6.2	6.1	6.0	5.9	5.9
1	12.8	10.3	9.1	8.3	7.8	7.4	7.2	7.0	6.8	6.7	6.6	6.5	6.4	6.3	6.2	6.2
2	13.1	10.6	9.4	8.6	8.1	7.7	7.5	7.3	7.1	7.0	6.9	6.8	6.7	6.6	6.5	6.5
3	13.4	10.9	9.7	8.9	8,4	8,0	7,8	7,6	7.4	7,3	7.2	7.1	7.0	6.9	6.8	6,8
4	13.7	11.2	10.0	9.2	8.7	8.3	8.1	7.9	7.7	7.6	7.5	7.4	7.3	7.2	7.1	7.1
5	14.0	11.5	10.3	9.5	9.0	8.6	8.4	8.2	8.0	7.9	7.8	7.7	7.6	7.5	7.4	7.4
6	14.3	11.8	10.6	9.8	9.3	8.9	8.7	8.5	8.3	8.2	8.1	8.0	7.9	7.8	7.7	7.7
7	14.6	12.1	10.9	10.1	9.6	9.2	9.0	8.8	8.6	8.5	8.4	8.3	8.2	8.1	8.0	8.0
8	14.9	12.4	11.2	10.4	9.9	9.5	9.3	9.1	8.9	8.8	8.7	8.6	8.5	8.4	8.3	8.3
9	15.2	12.7	11.5	10.7	10.2	9.8	9.6	9.4	9.2	9.1	9.0	8.9	8.8	8.7	8.6	8.6
10	15.5	13.0	11.8	11.0	10.5	10.1	9.9	9.7	9.5	9.4	9.3	9.2	9.1	9.0	8.9	8.9

$$R.A. = 0.3 \left(\frac{100 + S}{N} \right) + 5$$

Produced by West Lancashire Adult Basic Education Service (Skelmersdale College)

Appendix III
Reading Selections

Note: these levels are very approximate and will vary with individuals.

Selection	Approximate Level
Bob	Entry 2/3
Flying	Entry 3
First Day at School	Level 1
The Amazon Rainforest	Level 2(GCSE)
Chumley	Level 2 (GCSE)
Earthquake	(Post GCSE)
Hooliganism	(Post GCSE)
Everest	Advanced

Bob

When Bob grew up he was just the same. I kept hoping that he would begin to act like a normal person. He didn't. As he got older he got more odd, more crazy.

Bob spent most of his time going from job to job. Sometimes he would stick at a job for a few weeks. Sometimes he left after a few days. No one can live like that for long. You have to get a proper job. You need money to live.

When Bob was very hard up I used to give him a bit of money. Not much. Just a few pounds to keep him going. I felt sorry for him. Bob wasn't like other people. He didn't fit in. He wasn't a layabout. Not really. He was a bit mad. He couldn't help it. He was born that way.

Anyway Bob was my friend, I had to help him. He didn't have many friends. I was the only person he could go to when he was in trouble.

There was one thing that Bob really loved doing. He loved painting. I don't know much about painting. I was never any good at drawing or painting, but I could tell that Bob was good.

He did lots of paintings. He didn't ever sell them. He didn't make any money out of them. But they were good paintings. Bob put a lot of feeling into them. When I looked at those paintings I felt as if I could understand what was going on in Bob's mind. The paintings seemed to be part of him.

He always did paintings of places. Not real places. Just places he made up. Hills covered with trees. Fields of yellow corn. Yellow corn in the sunshine. Places like that. They were all in Bob's mind. He had never been to a place like that. He lived in the town and he didn't have the cash to go on holiday.

From The Ear *by Anita Jackson, reproduced by kind permission of Nelson Thornes Publishers Ltd*

Comprehension – Bob

1. Describe, in as much detail as you can remember, the passage you have just read.

   ....

   ....

   ....

2. What happened to Bob as he got older? ....

3. What did Bob do about a job? ....

4. Why did the author feel sorry for Bob? ....

5. What did the author think was good about Bob's paintings? ....

6. What did Bob paint? ....

7. What do you think Bob thought about money? ....

Flying

Afraid of flying? Well – yes and no, I suppose. I've been in a lot of dangerous situations, of course. Over Bolivia, for example. I was working for a small airline, and we carried just about everything, animals, whiskey, dynamite, and, of course, people. There were times when I felt I was flying a bomb, not a plane. Once, I was taking dynamite to the mines. Dynamite! Man, I have never seen so much. They had even put some on the floor right next to me. I was certainly nervous on that trip. Well, I was flying over mountains when suddenly the engine stopped. That time I landed without the plane. I got down all right, but I was hurt. I was lying there for about four days before they found me. They told me later that they had almost given me up for dead. Anyway, they got me back to hospital, and three months later I was flying again. No, I'm not afraid of flying. But there's a lot to worry about as pilot.

You know, flying the big planes over here in Europe isn't really less dangerous than flying those small planes in Bolivia. Near the airports there's such a lot of traffic. Only last week, I had just flown over from New York and was landing at Frankfurt airport. Suddenly I saw a small plane in front of me. It was crossing the airport – right in front of me. There's nothing you can do then, at 150mph. Anyway, I was lucky that time. I hadn't been able to move a finger!

Source unknown

Comprehension – Flying

1. Describe, in as much detail as possible the passage you have just read.

   ....

   ....

   ....

   ....

2. When he worked in Bolivia, what sort of things did they carry?

   ....

3. Where did they put the dynamite?

   ....

4. What happened the time the engine of his plane stopped?

   ....

5. How long was it before he was found?

   ....

6. Was flying in Europe less dangerous than in Bolivia?

   ....

7. What happened at Frankfurt airport?

   ....

8. Is this pilot afraid of flying?

   ....

First Day at School

I can remember my first day at the infant school quite well. My mother took me down to the gate of the school, big black iron gates with rust flaking off the bars. There was a huge cedar tree in the grounds, which was propped up by a pair of wooden telegraph poles. I never went too close to it then because I was never quite sure whether telegraph poles were very strong. As we went in, we were greeted by a smell of clay, paint and plimsolls, and earlier I had asked my mother what the rubber toecaps were for. She said that they were to protect your feet. So as I went into school, I kicked the doorframe as hard as I could and discovered to my distaste that they didn't really at all.

Later on, I was taken, with my mother, to see the Headmistress as were all newcomers. Looking out of the window, I saw what I thought was a walking stick on the roof. It turned out to be the top end of a fire-escape ladder.

Then my mother went home and I was taken into a classroom with lots of other little boys and girls, all engaged in painting things or doing things in the sand-pit, or knocking down other people's brick buildings. I found a wooden set of farm animals, and broke the donkey. Our classroom had large windows, with strange things outside. These were 'The Apparatus' which we were to climb on during P.E.

The teacher was a friendly person who showed us where things were and where to get milk. I hated milk. Once I was forced to drink it, or rather the teacher left me the milk with a quarter of an hour to get rid of it. It ended up being poured in the sand-pit.

When it was dinner-time, everyone went home except some of the boys and me. I went off to the dining-hall with the others. We had to go up a sloping corridor called 'The Link' and through a place where there is a notice displayed: 'This is the Quiet Part of the School', and then into the dining-hall. There were rows and rows of trestle-tables and benches. There was a ghastly smell of school dinner type stew and cleaning polish.

After dinner, we did some spelling, and I got my question right which made me most pleased with myself. My mother turned up in the doorway, and I explained to her that plimsolls do not protect your feet, that there was a walking-stick on the roof, and I got about twelve questions right. On the way home I was a dustman because I had my cap on just like dustmen do (back to front). I was proud to be a schoolboy.

Source unknown

Comprehension – First Day at School

1. Describe, in as much detail as you can remember, the passage you have just read.

   ....

   ....

   ....

   ....

2. Describe the gates of the school.

   ....

3. What did the boy's mother tell him the rubber toecaps on his plimsolls were for?

   ....

4. What's the first thing the boy did in the classroom?

   ....

5. How did he feel about drinking his milk?

   ....

6. Where did he eat dinner? What did he have?

   ....

7. What happened during spelling?

   ....

8. On the way home, how did he pretend he was a dustman?

   ....

The Amazon Rainforest

My speciality is insects. Ever since I was a boy I was fascinated by insects. A colourful and pretty beetle called 'joanina' (ladybird) was my favourite. I used to capture and collect them. That early boyhood love explains why I chose to become an entomologist, which is a person who studies insects.

As I enjoy catching insects and studying how they live, I'm lucky to be working in the rich Amazon rainforest where about one-third of the world's million or so species of insects live. Because there's a shortage of entomologists in the world, a complete study of the Amazon insects has yet to be done. We still have lots to learn, but our time is running out.

Some scientists say that in a few years time, the forests and jungles of the Amazon region will no longer exist, because they are being so rapidly destroyed by men who are building roads and housing settlements with no thought of protecting the natural habitat.

I am one of a group of about 250 scientists from many parts of the world who work together with Brazilians to research and study the fauna and flora of the Amazon.

A few years ago, when I was working for an examination, I had to observe communities of insects inside the rainforest. I found an old abandoned farmhouse near a stream and spent one week every month for a whole year working there. I gathered insects, including microscopic ones, from the rocks, tree trunks, fallen leaves, water and sand. Sometimes I had to dive into the streams with a mask and snorkel to find certain species.

One night in this lonely place in the dark jungle, there was a big storm with thunder and lightning. For the first time in my life I was really scared. I felt totally powerless and began to understand why the Indians, who live in the forest, feared these forces of nature and treated them like gods.

Source unknown

Comprehension – The Amazon Rainforest

1. Describe, in as much detail as you can remember, the passage you have just read.

   ....

   ....

   ....

   ....

2. What is the author's job?

   ....

3. What was his favourite insect when he was a boy?

   ....

4. Where does he work?

   ....

5. How many species of insects are there in the world?

   ....

6. Why do some scientists think the Amazon rainforest will soon no longer exist?

   ....

7. Where did he stay when he was working for an examination?

   ....

8. What effect did being alone in the jungle storm have on him?

   ....

Chumley

Chumley was a full-grown chimpanzee. His owner, a District Officer, was finding the ape's large size rather awkward and he wanted to send him to London Zoo as a present, so that he could visit the animal when he was back in England on leave. He wrote asking us if we would mind taking Chumley back with us when we left and depositing him at his new home in London and we replied that we would not mind at all.

He arrived in the back of a small van, seated sedately in a huge crate. When the doors of this crate were opened and Chumley stepped out with all the ease and self-confidence of a film star, I was considerably shaken, for, standing on his bow legs in a normal slouching chimp position, he came up to my waist, and if he had straightened up, his head would have been on a level with my chest. He had huge arms, and must have measured at least twice my measurements round his hairy chest. Owing to bad tooth growth both sides of his face were swollen out of all proportion, and this gave him a weird, pugilistic look. His eyes were small, deep-set, and intelligent. The top of his head was nearly bald owing, I discovered later, to his habit of sitting and rubbing the palm of his hand backward across his head, an exercise which seemed to afford him much pleasure and which he persisted in until the top of his skull was quite devoid of hair. This was no young chimp as I had expected, but a veteran of about eight or nine years old, fully mature, strong as a powerful man, and to judge by his expression, with considerable experience of life. Although he was not exactly a nice chimp to look at (I had seen more handsome), he certainly had a striking personality: it hit you as soon as you set eyes on him. His little eyes looked at you with great intelligence and there seemed to be a glitter of ironic laughter in their depths that made you feel uncomfortable.

I sat down opposite him and produced a packet of cigarettes. As I was selecting, one long black arm was stretched across the table, and Chumley grunted in delight. Wondering what he would do, I handed him a cigarette, and to my astonishment he put it carefully in the corner of his mouth. I lit my smoke and handed him the matches thinking that this would fool him. He opened the box, took out a match, struck it, lit his cigarette, threw the matches down on the table, crossed his legs again and lay back in his chair inhaling thankfully and blowing clouds of smoke out of his nose.

From The Overloaded Ark *by Gerald Durrell, reproduced by kind permission of Faber & Faber Ltd*

Comprehension – Chumley

1. Describe, in as much detail as you can remember, the passage you have just read.

   ....

   ....

   ....

   ....

2. Where was Chumley being sent? Why?

   ....

3. Describe Chumley physically.

   ....

4. Describe Chumley's personality.

   ....

5. Why was Chumley bald?

   ....

6. How old was he?

   ....

7. Describe the incident with the cigarettes.

   ....

8. What things about Chumley surprised the author?

   ....

Earthquake

The earthquake had done little to clear the air. It was as hot as ever. In the animal world there seemed some strange commotion, as if they had wind of something. The usual lizards and mosquitoes were still absent; but in their place the earth's most horrid progeny, creatures of darkness, sought the open; land-crabs wandered about aimlessly, angrily twiddling their claws; and the ground seemed almost alive with red ants and cockroaches. Up on the roof the pigeons were gathered, talking to each other fearfully.

It was the custom that, whenever their father had been to St. Anne's, John and Emily should run out to meet him, and ride back with him, one perched on each of his stirrups.

That Sunday evening they ran out as soon as they saw him coming, in spite of the thunderstorm that by now was clattering over their heads – and not only over their heads either, for in the tropics a thunderstorm is not a remote affair up in the sky, as it is in England, but it is all round you; lightning plays ducks and drakes across the water, bounds from tree to tree, bounces about the ground, while the thunder seems to proceed from violent explosions in your own very core.

'Go back! Go back, you damned little fools!', he yelled furiously; 'Get into the house!'

They stopped, aghast; and began to realise that after all it was a storm of more than usual violence. They discovered that they were drenched to the skin – must have been the moment they left the house. The lightning kept up a continuous blaze; it was playing about their father's very stirrup-irons and all of a sudden they realised he was afraid. They fled to the house, shocked to the heart and he was in the house almost as soon as they were. Mrs Thornton rushed out:

'My dear, I'm so glad . . .'

'I've never seen such a storm! Why on earth did you let the children come out?

'I never dreamt they would be so silly! and all the time I was thinking – but thank Heaven you're back!'

'I think the worst is over now'.

Perhaps it was; but all through supper the lightning shone almost without flickering. And John and Emily could hardly eat; the memory of that momentary look on their father's face haunted them.

From High Wind in Jamaica, *by Richard Hughes, published by Random House, reproduced by kind permission of David Higham Associates Ltd.*

Comprehension – Earthquake

1. Describe, in as much detail as you remember, the passage you have just read.

   ....

   ....

   ....

   ....

2. What had happened as a result of the earthquake?

   ....

3. How were the animals affected?

   ....

4. Where does the story take place?

   ....

5. What are the children's names?

   ....

6. Why was their father angry?

   ....

7. How was this storm different from others?

   ....

8. What scared the children most?

   ....

Hooliganism

Undoubtedly the most damaging aspect of our football at the moment is hooliganism. Other facets of the matter may be debated; this violence is solely harmful. Mr Dennis Follows, when he was secretary of the Football Association, diagnosed it accurately when he advocated the banning of spectators under the age of eighteen from football grounds.

His idea was rejected for valid human reasons. Saturday has replaced the old Sunday morning as the working man's time of glory. The football match, core of Saturday, is, for many orderly youthful citizens as well as the unruly, the compensation for a week of monotonous, depressing work and, often, dispiriting family life. Mr Follows identified the specifically disruptive adolescent element.

On the other hand, many of his critics appeared to think that the youngsters in question were simply football followers enthusiastically supporting their own teams. If that were the whole matter it would be relatively easy to adjust; but it is not. Apparently it is not generally realized that many of these young men drink heavily on their football match 'day out'. The youngest of them – quite early teenagers – can be seen buying drink in the public-houses near many of the large grounds; it is simpler, safer, and more profitable for publicans to serve them than to ask their age or refuse. It may be accepted from one who has now twice been forced to defend himself against their mindless violence, that a mob of drunken fifteen- or sixteen-year-olds is frighteningly illogical, unpredictable, and potentially violent.

A significant statistic of public reaction shows that in a recent year Boxing Day attendances at League matches were 300,000 lower than in the previous year. This, on a fine day for the season, could not be explained away by the postponement of one Second and one Fourth Division match, the general quality of play, or competition from television.

The effect of hooliganism is almost certainly wider than has generally been accepted. It is not limited to driving away spectators who used to watch from the terraces, who are not prepared to take the risk of violence there, but cannot afford grandstand seats. It is increasingly clear that a considerable number of people, who used to travel by train to 'their' team's away matches or from areas without first-class football, no longer do so because of the atmosphere created by young supporters in trains and at railway stations.

Source unknown

Comprehension – Hooliganism

1. Describe, in as much detail as you remember, the passage you have just read.

   ....

   ....

   ....

   ....

2. Who is, or was, Dennis Follows?

   ....

3. What did he advocate?

   ....

4. Why was his idea rejected?

   ....

5. What is the problem?

   ....

6. Why don't publicans refuse to serve the young men?

   ....

7. What is public reaction to hooliganism?

   ....

8. What statistic does the author quote?

   ....

9. What other effects of hooliganism have there been?

   ....

Everest

The rarefied air surrounding the upper part of Everest, or any other of the big peaks, obviously makes movement, even over easy ground, much more difficult. Lack of oxygen also slows down and blurs the mental processes. Beyond a certain point life itself is no longer possible. On the other hand, it is now sufficiently proved that the ill-effects of altitude on the climber may at least be retarded by a careful regimen of what we call acclimatization, a gradual getting used to increased height over a certain period of time. Individual performances on a mountain naturally vary but it may be said that those among us who are best adapted to climb high mountains, provided they follow this policy of gradualness, can reach an altitude of at least 21,000 feet and remain there without serious detriment – at any rate long enough to make a supreme final effort to reach a higher point, provided it is not too far above.

Trouble begins above that height, which is one main reason why the really high peaks – those of 26,000 feet and over – are in a different category of difficulty from any lesser ones. The policy of gradualness breaks down, for the muscle tissues begin to deteriorate fairly rapidly and the climber's resistance to cold, his fortitude in the face of wind and weather, are weakened. He tends to lose the promptings of appetite and thirst and he is denied the relaxation of normal sleep. In fact, from about 21,000 feet onwards, he really needs greatly to speed up the rate of his progress and employ 'rush' tactics. But this he cannot do. On the contrary, he is increasingly handicapped by the height as he climbs and his progress becomes painfully slow; the mental effort, like the physical, is infinitely greater. If this is true of easy ground, it is the more so when difficulties arise, even minor ones which would not deter a moderate performer at a lower height. A slight change of gradient may be a straw which will break the camel's back. Considering that Everest is over 29,000 feet and that some 8,000 feet have to be climbed above this established level of successful acclimatization, one aspect of our problem, which also played an important part in defeating former expeditions, becomes clear.

From The Ascent of Everest *by Sir John Hunt,*
reproduced by kind permission of Hodder & Stoughton Ltd

Comprehension – Everest

1. Describe, in as much detail as you can remember, the passage you have just read.

   ....

   ....

   ....

   ....

2. Why is movement on the upper part of Everest more difficult?

   ....

3. What is acclimatization?

   ....

4. Why does a climber acclimatize himself?

   ....

5. At what height does trouble begin for a climber?

   ....

6. What happens to a climber beyond this height?

   ....

7. What should a climber do to achieve the climb?

   ....

8. What explanation does the author give for why former expeditions have been defeated?

   ....

Irregular Words

Pilot Version *(These should be read across the page)*

who	one	their	eye	
school	only	give	people	
walk	know	light	enough	
front	once	sign	thought	
heard	calm	island	debt	
eight	ghastly	biscuit	choir	
science	worst	orchestra	yacht	borough
grotesque	weird	headache	colonel	phlegm

Alison Swabey, London Language & Literacy Unit, 2002

The Irregular Word List

ache	placebo	debt	facade	psalm
gauche	chord	banal	bouquet	deny
heir	equivocal	aisle	quadruped	subtle
nausea	superfluous	naive	zealot	thyme
aeon	courteous	gaoled	hiatus	gist
simile	rarefy	procreate	cellist	gouge

Long Regular Words

adventurously	chitterling	individual
herpetology	uninterested	fleeringly
experimenter	huckaback	apprehensive
intertergal	indiscoverable	tipularian
manufactured	gressorial	organisations
pegmatitic	particularly	hectographic
masterpiece	shibboleth	

Nelson, Hazel E., 'New Adult Reading Test', Test Manual, 1977.

The Snowling Graded Non-word Reading Test (Revised Pilot Version)

Name ....

Practice samples

fer ....   mot ....

wut ....   kib ....

hin...

One-syllable items

1. mosp ....   6. gromp ....

2. kisp ....   7. snid ....

3. drant ....   8. hast ....

4. prab ....   9. trolb ....

5. sted ....   10. twesk ....

Two-syllable items

1. hinshink ....   6. tegwop ....

2. molsmit......................................   7. balras ....

3. nolcrid..   8. chamgalp ....

4. twamket ....   9. kipthirm ....

5. stansert ....   10. sloskon ....

Observations

....

....

....

Score

One-syllable...

Two-syllable ....

Courtesy of Dr Margaret Snowling. See Resources for the updated version.

118

Appendix V

Spelling Dictation Example

Diagnostic Three

One night my friend woke me, saying, 'Would you enjoy a trial run in my new helicopter?' I had scarcely scrambled into my tracksuit before we were away. The lights of the city glowed beneath, and the stars shone above. I was beginning to wonder about our destination. Then I caught sight of the spinning knife edge and the surface of a flying saucer whistling round. We dodged skilfully in order to avoid an accident. To our relief, the spacecraft regained height and we sank down to earth. I woke in my comfortable bed which I had never actually left.

from Spelling in Context *by Margaret Peters and Brigid Smith, reproduced by kind permission of NFER-NELSON.*

Diagnostic dictations level 1, 2 and 4 can be found in Spelling in Context *by Margaret Peters and Brigid Smith.*

Advanced Spelling List

intelligible	temporarily
innumerable	curiosity
unconscionable	convenience
antecedent	conveyance
acquittal	abstinence
occurrence	catastrophe
sarcasm	beneficial
righteous	luxuriate
illustration	typhoid
triumph	pageant
deprecate	intrusion
personnel	visibility
compensatory	tyrannical
courtesy	remunerative

Spoonerism Task: Segmenting Sounds

This is an oral task. Ask the person to transpose the initial sound of each word to create a 'spoonerism', e.g. *John Lennon* becomes *Lon Jennon*.

A non-dyslexic adult will usually take between one and two minutes to complete the task. Dyslexic adults may struggle to do them and may not be able to do some at all. If they are able to do them, they will take much longer, up to several minutes. If the individual is finding it very difficult, you do not need to complete the list.

Jack Dee	Henry James
Kate Moss	David Beckham
Tom Hanks	Buddy Holly
Robin Cook	Mick Jagger
Walt Disney	Richard Burton
Mel Gibson	Julia Roberts
Tony Benn	Kylie Minogue
Bob Marley	Harrison Ford
Mike Tyson	Billie Piper
Tiger Woods	Charles Dickens

Resources

To order *Access for All* and other curriculum documents contact:
The Basic Skills Agency
Admail 524, London
WC1A 1BR
Tel: 0870 600 2400
Fax: 0870 600 2401
www.basic-skills.co.uk

For information about the *Learning Materials* and the *Diagnostic Assessment Materials* contact:
Adult Basic Skills Strategy Unit
Department for Education and Skills
Level 1, Caxton House
Tothill Street
London
SW1H 9NF
www.dfes.gov.uk/readwriteplus/publications

For a list of specialist optometrists and a kit of overlays with instructions for screening:
Cerium Visual Technologies
Cerium Technology Park
Tenterden
Kent
TN30 7DE
Tel: 01580 765 211
www.ceriumvistech.co.uk

For a Dyslexia Adult Screening Test (DAST):

The Psychological Corporation

Harcourt Education

Halley Court

Jordan Hill

Oxford

OX2 8EJ

Tel: 01865 888 188

www.tpc-international.com

For specialist dyslexia assessment of vision:

Institute of Optometry

56-62 Newington Causeway

London

SE1 6DS

Tel: 020 7403 4183

www.ioo.org.uk

For the *Graded Non-word Reading Test*, Snowling, Stothard and McLean:

Thames Valley Test Company

Unit 22

The Granary

Station Road

Thurston

Bury St Edmonds

Suffolk

IP31 3QU

Tel: 01359 232 941

The following are available from Avanti:

Avanti Books
8 Parsons Green
Boulton Road
Stevenage
SG1 4QG
Tel: 01438 350 155
www.avantibooks.com

Brown, H. and Brown, M. *Use Your Eyes*, Brown & Brown, 1992, 2nd edition (for useful tasks of visual recognition of shapes, letters and words).

Identifying Dyslexia: a diagnostic interview, Spelling to Learn: using a learning styles approach to spelling with dyslexic adults, and *On Being Dyslexic: adults talking about dyslexia* (Adult Dyslexia Video Series), London Language & Literacy Unit.

Sunderland, H., Klein, C., Savinson, R., Partridge, T., *Dyslexia and the Bilingual Learner: Assessing and teaching young people and adults who speak English as an additional language*, London Language & Literacy Unit, 1997

Other useful contacts and resources:

Bangor Dyslexia Test, Learning Development Aids

Helen Irlen Centres UK
http://www.irlen.co.uk

Goodwin, V. and Thomson, B., *Adult Students and Dyslexia: a resource book for adult dyslexics and staff*, Open University, 1995 (contains digit span test).